VOLUME 9

NEW TESTAMENT

THE NEW COLLEGEVILLE BIBLE COMMENTARY

FIRST AND SECOND TIMOTHY, TITUS, PHILEMON

Terence J. Keegan, O.P.

SERIES EDITOR

Daniel Durken, O.S.B.

LITURGICAL PRESS
Collegeville, Minnesota

www.litpress.org

Nihil obstat: Robert C. Harren, *Censor deputatus.*
Imprimatur: ✠ John F. Kinney, Bishop of St. Cloud, Minnesota, December 29, 2005.

Design by Ann Blattner.

Cover illustration: *Paul's Life* by Donald Jackson. Natural hand-ground ink on calf-skin vellum, 15-7/8" x 24-1/2". Copyright 2005 *The Saint John's Bible* and the Hill Museum & Manuscript Library at Saint John's University, United States of America. Scripture quotations are from the New Revised Standard Version of the Bible, Catholic Edition, copyright © 1989, 1993 National Council of the Churches of Christ in the United States of America. Used by permission. All rights reserved.

Photos: page 8, David Manahan, O.S.B.; pages 36 and 56, Corel Photos.

Scriptures selections are taken from the New American Bible Copyright © 1991, 1986, 1970 by the Confraternity of Christian Doctrine, 3211 Fourth Street, NE, Washington, DC 20017-1194 and are used by license of copyright owner. All rights reserved. No part of the New American Bible may be reproduced in any form or by any means without permission in writing from the copyright owner.

1	2	3	4	5	6	7	8	9

Library of Congress Cataloging-in-Publication Data

Keegan, Terence J.
    First Timothy, Second Timothy, Titus, Philemon / Terence J. Keegan.
      p. cm. — (New Collegeville Bible commentary. New Testament ; v. 9)
    Summary: "Complete biblical texts with sound, scholarly based commentary that is written at a pastoral level; the Scripture translation is that of the New American Bible with Revised New Testament and Revised Psalms (1991)" —Provided by publisher.
    ISBN-13: 978-0-8146-2868-3 (pbk. : alk. paper)
    ISBN-10: 0-8146-2868-0 (pbk. : alk. paper)
    1. Bible. N.T. Pastoral epistles—Commentaries. 2. Bible. N.T. Philemon—Commentaries. I. Title. II. Series.

BS2735.53.K44   2005
227'.83077—dc22

                                              2004030301

CONTENTS

ABBREVIATIONS

Books of the Bible

Acts—Acts of the Apostles
Amos—Amos
Bar—Baruch
1 Chr—1 Chronicles
2 Chr—2 Chronicles
Col—Colossians
1 Cor—1 Corinthians
2 Cor—2 Corinthians
Dan—Daniel
Deut—Deuteronomy
Eccl (or Qoh)—Ecclesiastes
Eph—Ephesians
Esth—Esther
Exod—Exodus
Ezek—Ezekiel
Ezra—Ezra
Gal—Galatians
Gen—Genesis
Hab—Habakkuk
Hag—Haggai
Heb—Hebrews
Hos—Hosea
Isa—Isaiah
Jas—James
Jdt—Judith
Jer—Jeremiah
Job—Job
Joel—Joel
John—John
1 John—1 John
2 John—2 John
3 John—3 John
Jonah—Jonah
Josh—Joshua
Jude—Jude
Judg—Judges
1 Kgs—1 Kings

2 Kgs—2 Kings
Lam—Lamentations
Lev—Leviticus
Luke—Luke
1 Macc—1 Maccabees
2 Macc—2 Maccabees
Mal—Malachi
Mark—Mark
Matt—Matthew
Mic—Micah
Nah—Nahum
Neh—Nehemiah
Num—Numbers
Obad—Obadiah
1 Pet—1 Peter
2 Pet—2 Peter
Phil—Philippians
Phlm—Philemon
Prov—Proverbs
Ps(s)—Psalms
Rev—Revelation
Rom—Romans
Ruth—Ruth
1 Sam—1 Samuel
2 Sam—2 Samuel
Sir—Sirach
Song—Song of Songs
1 Thess—1 Thessalonians
2 Thess—2 Thessalonians
1 Tim—1 Timothy
2 Tim—2 Timothy
Titus—Titus
Tob—Tobit
Wis—Wisdom
Zech—Zechariah
Zeph—Zephaniah

The First Letter to Timothy

The First Letter to Timothy is the first of three letters usually referred to as the Pastoral Letters because they deal with matters concerning the leadership and organization of the Christian community. While some think that Paul may have composed 2 Timothy and possibly the others as well, most scholars believe that they come from a period after the death of Paul, probably composed by followers of Paul who were concerned that his legacy be handed on to the next generation of Christians. The practice of ascribing later writings to an earlier major figure was common in the ancient world; it can be found in the writings of the Old Testament and other ancient Jewish writings, as well as in the literature of ancient Greece and Rome.

Regardless of who wrote them, all agree that these letters are presented as having the authority of Paul and that they are generally consistent with themes that appear in other Pauline letters. Ultimately, however, the question of authorship does not affect their authoritative status, for, whoever wrote them, they are part of the inspired scriptural conversation between God and God's people.

Similarities among all three Pastoral Letters have led many scholars to consider them together when dealing with questions of authorship as well as interpretation. While there are striking similarities between 1 Timothy and Titus, there are striking differences between these two and 2 Timothy. 1 Timothy and Titus were written in an ancient letter form known as "commandments of a ruler," a letter from a ruler to a delegate and his community. Both of these letters deal with leadership roles in the community, the responsibilities of various groups within the community, and the threat of some kind of Jewish Christian false teaching. 2 Timothy deals with none of these matters but instead is a personal letter exhorting Timothy, by imitating Paul, to be the person through whom authentic Pauline teaching is to be transmitted to future generations. It makes no mention of offices within the community or the responsibilities of community members. Timothy is charged to combat false teaching, but the false teachings are nowhere described as Jewish.

While 2 Timothy may not have been written by Paul during his life, it was composed in the style of a distinctively Pauline letter and contains passages and biographical material that many feel are authentically Pauline. 1 Timothy and Titus depart in significant ways from the Pauline letter form, and their similarities indicate that they were composed probably subsequent to 2 Timothy and possibly by a different person or persons.

These three letters, like Philemon but unlike the other Pauline letters, are each addressed to a single person. The intended audience, however, is not just Timothy or Titus (the ones to whom these letters are addressed) but the larger Christian community (the implied reader). Paul had preached in all the communities to which he wrote letters, with the exception of the Roman community, and even there he was known to many members of the community and would shortly be visiting that community. Unlike these letters, the Pastoral Letters are addressed to church leaders and members of a later generation that may not have known Paul personally. Addressing these letters to Timothy and Titus not only suited the content and purpose of these letters (orderly succession of leaders and correctness of teaching) but also extended the authority of Paul, through persons known to him in his lifetime, to communities of a later generation.

Interestingly, Timothy and Titus are both presented as young men and are instructed to serve as models of behavior for young men in their communities (1 Tim 4:12; Titus 2:7). The historical figures were indeed young men when Paul first encountered them early in his ministry. They would have been much older toward the end of Paul's ministry, where some scholars attempt to locate the Pastoral Letters.

Timothy appears in all of Paul's undisputed letters except Galatians and frequently appears in the Acts of the Apostles. He is listed as Paul's coauthor in most of the letters that include a coauthor (2 Cor 1:1; Phil 1:1; Col 1:1; 1 Thess 1:1; 2 Thess 1:1; Phlm 1). Titus appears only in 2 Corinthians and Galatians. They both appear as trusted companions of Paul, true to his teachings. "For this reason I am sending you Timothy, who is my beloved and faithful son in the Lord; he will remind you of my ways in Christ [Jesus], just as I teach them everywhere in every church" (1 Cor 4:17). "As for Titus, he is my partner and co-worker for you . . ." (2 Cor 8:23).

According to the narrative of 1 Timothy, Paul had gone to Macedonia, leaving Timothy temporarily in charge of the community at Ephesus. At some later date, whether in Macedonia or elsewhere, he wrote to Timothy, charging him to fulfill his responsibilities until he, Paul, returned. In detailing Timothy's responsibilities, the letter deals with the organization of the community, the roles of its leaders and all the other members of the community. It also explains how to handle the problem of false teachers, including those who, in their asceticism and renunciation of marriage, claimed Paul as their champion. While both 1 Timothy and Titus deal with false teachings and church order, in 1 Timothy the false teachings are more complex and the church organization further developed.

One of the reasons so many scholars are convinced that 1 Timothy was written long after the death of Paul is that it, like Titus, seems to address a period in the development of the early church when concern is for settled order and correct transmission of doctrine. The great Pauline themes of faith, righteousness, and grace, in dynamic development in Paul's early letters, appear here in fixed formulas. The apostolic and charismatic leadership of the early church is past, and the present need is for order, discipline, and virtue in a stable church structure. These letters shift away from Paul's perspective on believers living in a world that is in tension with the coming age. They appropriate the Pauline tradition for a new situation to refute false teachers and to establish the church as the kind of community that can carry the Pauline tradition forward into future generations. The shift apparent in these letters is somewhat comparable to that called for in the document The Church in the Modern World issued by the Second Vatican Council, calling on the church to become more fully engaged with contemporary secular society.

The emphasis of 1 Timothy on God's universal saving intention (2:4-6; see also Titus 2:11-14), as well as its positive view of creation (4:3-4), served to bring the Pauline gospel into the mainstream of contemporary society. While its moral vision of the compatibility of the ethics of church with that of society is somewhat at odds with the perspective of social alienation found in the book of Revelation, both of these parts of the New Testament, each in its own way, challenge the contemporary reader to find ways in which to engage society without betraying the integrity of the gospel message.

The First Letter to Timothy

I. Address

1 **Greeting.** ¹Paul, an apostle of Christ Jesus by command of God our savior and of Christ Jesus our hope, ²to Timothy, my true child in faith: grace, mercy, and peace from God the Father and Christ Jesus our Lord.

II. Sound Teaching

Warning against False Doctrine. ³I ▶ repeat the request I made of you when I was on my way to Macedonia, that you stay in Ephesus to instruct certain people not to teach false doctrines ⁴or to concern themselves with myths and

---

1:1-2 The opening

Ancient letters usually began with an identification of the sender and the recipient, followed by a short greeting. This letter begins by identifying its sender, "Paul"; his position, "apostle of Christ Jesus"; and the source of his authority, "God our savior and Christ Jesus our hope." This way of identifying the sender also focuses on an important theme both of this letter and of the letter to Titus—the theme of hope. In this letter and especially in Titus, God is the ground and object of hope, which is fulfilled in the gift of eternal life (1 Tim 4:10). God is the source of hope insofar as he saves us by being faithful to the divine promises, sending Christ Jesus to redeem us and form us into a chosen people (Titus 2:14).

The recipient is identified as "Timothy, my true child in faith." This expression illustrates an understanding of the church as a genuinely new family that needs to be nurtured and protected as it grows and matures, as well as designating Timothy as the legitimate representative authorized to minister in Paul's name. The expression "true child" is also used of Titus in the letter addressed to him (Titus 1:4), but in 2 Timothy, Timothy is addressed as "dear child" (2 Tim 1:2). The language in 1 Timothy and Titus emphasizes the authentication of Timothy and Titus. They are teachers in whom communities can put their trust. The greeting expands the typical

---

▶ This symbol indicates a cross reference number in the *Catechism of the Catholic Church*. See page 79 for number citations.

9

Detail of a Roman sarcophagus in the area of Pergamum in Asia Minor

endless genealogies, which promote speculations rather than the plan of God that is to be received by faith. ⁵The aim of this instruction is love from a pure heart, a good conscience, and a sincere faith. ⁶Some people have deviated from these and turned to meaningless talk, ⁷wanting to be teachers of the law, but without understanding either what they are saying or what they assert with such assurance.

⁸We know that the law is good, provided that one uses it as law, ⁹with the understanding that law is meant not

---

Pauline greeting, "grace and peace," by the addition of "mercy," perhaps in anticipation of the stress on mercy in the thanksgiving at 1:13.

SETTING THE CONTEXT

I Tim 1:3-11

1:3-7 Defend against false teaching

As Paul goes off to Macedonia, Timothy is left behind in Ephesus and given responsibility to exercise leadership in Paul's absence. While in 2 Timothy Paul entrusts his gospel to Timothy (2 Tim 1:14; 2:2), in 1 Timothy it is Paul to whom the gospel has been entrusted (1:11; 2:7). Paul remains in control and continues to exercise his responsibilities (3:14; 4:13). Timothy, as his representative, is charged to counter with correct instruction the false teaching that has arisen at Ephesus. The purpose of the instruction, however, is not simply to negate the false teaching but to "love from a pure heart, a good conscience, and a sincere faith" (1:5). Here, as elsewhere in 1 Timothy and Titus, there is a clear connection made between correct doctrine and a morally and religiously integrated life.

The "myths and endless genealogies" (1:4) that are being taught by these "teachers of the law" (1:7) are probably the same as what the letter to Titus calls "Jewish myths and regulations of people" (Titus 1:14). Some think that "genealogies" (1:4; see Titus 3:9) in the false teachings indicate some kind of gnostic speculation. More likely, however, they concern speculations on the lineage of the patriarchs. Here and in Titus there is lack of specificity on these false teachings, both because there is no need to provide a hearing for dangerous opinions and because the real point of the letters is to promote a well-integrated life for members of well-ordered communities.

1:8-11 The value and function of the law

The law referred to in these verses is the Jewish Law, concerning which Paul had said, "a person is not justified by works of the law but through faith in Jesus Christ" (Gal 2:16). Nevertheless, he also maintained

for a righteous person but for the lawless and unruly, the godless and sinful, the unholy and profane, those who kill their fathers or mothers, murderers, ◀ ¹⁰the unchaste, sodomites, kidnapers, liars, perjurers, and whatever else is opposed to sound teaching, ¹¹according to the glorious gospel of the blessed God, with which I have been entrusted.

Gratitude for God's Mercy. ¹²I am grateful to him who has strengthened

---

that "the law is holy, and the commandment is holy and righteous and good" (Rom 7:12). The law was able to point out sinfulness, although it lacked the power to save. 1 Timothy 1:8-11 is saying essentially what Paul had said. A concern of this letter is with those who continue to oppose Paul by imposing Jewish legal obligations or who misrepresent Paul by teaching a kind of libertinism that gives free rein to all kinds of behavior.

These verses employ a common feature of popular moral preaching, namely, a listing of typical vices. The list here is based on the core of the Old Testament law, the Ten Commandments. The vices listed are said to be opposed to "sound teaching" (1:10; 4:6), which, like "sound words" (6:3), refers in 1 Timothy and Titus to the kind of teaching that leads to correct moral behavior (see Titus 1:9, 13; 2:1, 2, 8).

OPENING BRACKET

I Tim 1:12-20

This passage and another similar passage near the end of the letter (6:11-16, 20-21a) bracket the body of the letter (2:1–6:10, 17-19). These bracketing passages focus on the overall purpose of the letter: the entrusting of Paul's gospel to Timothy for the purpose of protecting it from false teachers. In the opening bracket more emphasis is placed on Christ Jesus appointing Paul to his ministry (1:12), while the closing bracket emphasizes Timothy's responsibility to guard what has been entrusted to him (6:20) "until the appearance of our Lord Jesus Christ" (6:14). Both, however, focus on the charge entrusted to Timothy (1:18; 6:20), both times using the Greek vocative case (indicating the person addressed, "Timothy"), a case rarely used in the New Testament and used only these two times in this letter, a clear indication of their parallel and bracketing function.

In both passages Timothy's responsibilities are set in the context of community attestation: "prophetic words" (1:18) and "many witnesses" (6:12). In both Timothy is encouraged with metaphors of competition: to "fight a good fight" (1:18) and to "compete well for the faith" (6:12). In both Timothy is warned about the dangerous opposition that threatens the faith (1:19-20;

me, Christ Jesus our Lord, because he considered me trustworthy in appointing me to the ministry. [13]I was once a blasphemer and a persecutor and an arrogant man, but I have been mercifully treated because I acted out of ignorance in my unbelief. [14]Indeed, the grace of our Lord has been abundant, along with the faith and love that are in Christ Jesus. [15]This saying is trust- ▶

6:21). The special bracketing function of these passages is further highlighted by the fact that both include a doxology, an act of praise (1:17; 6:15-16). Both doxologies emphasize the uniqueness of God: "the only God" (1:17) and "the only ruler" (6:15), which provides the basis for the letter's emphasis on universal salvation (2:3-6). God's desire that all be saved is the reason why Paul was appointed an apostle (2:7) and the reason why Timothy is being charged to defend Paul's gospel in the face of opposition.

1:12-17 Prayer of thanksgiving

Pauline letters typically have a passage immediately after the opening in which Paul gives thanks to God for what God has done for the community or person to whom the letter is addressed. While 2 Timothy has the characteristic Pauline thanksgiving (2 Tim 1:3-5), it is lacking in both 1 Timothy and Titus. The belated thanksgiving in the present passage is addressed to Christ rather than to God, and the thanksgiving is for what Christ has done for Paul, not for what God has done for the letter's recipient. The present passage is actually more like the interjected thanksgivings in Paul's letters in which Paul thanks God for favors to himself (Rom 7:25; 1 Cor 15:57).

This thanksgiving, as part of the opening bracket, does serve as a foundation for the main themes of the letter and is appropriately placed after the passages that deal with false teaching and immorality. Paul himself was "once a blasphemer and a persecutor and an arrogant man" (1:13). Subsequently, by grace and faith, he became a Christian leader and "an example for those who would come to believe in [Christ]" (1:16). Paul serves as an example for readers up to the present day of how "the grace of our Lord" (1:14) can transform even the most arrogant person into a servant of Christ. The remainder of the letter will continue these themes, that is, upright living that follows from correct understanding of Christian doctrine as well as the proper exercise of leadership and authority in the Christian community.

The Christian doctrine at the heart of this passage, "Christ Jesus came into the world to save sinners" (1:15), is introduced by "this saying is trustworthy," a phrase regularly used in the Pastoral Letters to identify a basic

worthy and deserves full acceptance: Christ Jesus came into the world to save sinners. Of these I am the foremost. [16]But for that reason I was mercifully treated, so that in me, as the foremost, Christ Jesus might display all his patience as an example for those who would come to believe in him for everlasting life. [17]To the king of ages, incorruptible, invisible, the only God, honor and glory forever and ever. Amen.

Responsibility of Timothy. [18]I entrust this charge to you, Timothy, my child, in accordance with the prophetic

---

truth of early Christian faith (1 Tim 3:1; 4:9; 2 Tim 2:11; Titus 3:8). The passage concludes with a doxology which, like the doxology found at the end of the letter (6:15-16), includes all four elements usually found in New Testament doxologies: the object of praise, "the king of ages, incorruptible, invisible, the only God"; an expression of praise, "honor and glory"; an indication of time, "forever and ever"; and a response, "Amen." Interestingly, while the thanksgiving is addressed to Christ Jesus (1:12), the doxology is addressed to God.

1:18-20 Timothy's responsibilities

The mention of Timothy's name in verse 18 is a departure from the style of letter writing in the Hellenistic world. Names of recipients would normally appear only in the opening and closing of the letter. Mention of his name at this point serves the bracketing function of this passage and refocuses the letter on Timothy (the recipient) after the thanksgiving has been focused on Paul, highlighting the seriousness of the challenge Timothy is facing in opposing error in the church. He is to take up this challenge "in accordance with the prophetic words once spoken about you" (1:18). Prophecy—words uttered by God's spokesperson—is the only charism that appears in all of Paul's lists of spiritual gifts (Rom 12:6; 1 Cor 12:10, 28, 29; see 1 Cor 13:2; 14:6, 22). Here and at 4:14 prophecy is associated with the charismatic authorization of Timothy's ministry, a ministry here described as fighting a good fight with the weapons of faith and a good conscience.

While the opponents Timothy is to deal with are never identified and their teaching is only vaguely described, two individuals are cited with whom Paul presumably had to deal. They are cited here as examples of the kinds of persons Timothy is to beware. Both names appear in 2 Timothy. Hymenaeus said that the resurrection has already taken place, (2 Tim 2:17-18), and Alexander the coppersmith did Paul a great deal of harm (2 Tim 4:14). Their use here may be an indication that 2 Timothy preceded and influenced 1 Timothy. Both men have been "handed over to Satan" (1:20), the procedure indicated for the incestuous man in 1 Corinthians 5:1-5. In both places the procedure—what today would be called excom-

words once spoken about you. Through them may you fight a good fight ¹⁹by having faith and a good conscience. Some, by rejecting conscience, have made a shipwreck of their faith, ²⁰among them Hymenaeus and Alexander, whom I have handed over to Satan to be taught not to blaspheme.

III. Problems of Discipline

2 **Prayer and Conduct.** ¹First of all, then, I ask that supplications, prayers, petitions, and thanksgivings be offered for everyone, ²for kings and for all in authority, that we may lead a quiet and tranquil life in all devotion and dignity. ³This is good and pleasing

---

munication—is not punitive but educative and should lead to conversion. A similar procedure appears in Titus 3:10-11. Support for this procedure emphasizes the overall concern of 1 Timothy and Titus with correct teaching and good order in the community.

THE HOUSEHOLD OF GOD

I Tim 2:1–3:15

2:1-7 Universal salvation and good citizenship

After the opening bracket, the four main sections of the letter deal with good order in the community, true devotion as opposed to false teaching, the responsibilities of Timothy as a community leader, and dealing with false teachers. False teaching threatens the stability of the community both in itself and with respect to the surrounding secular world. Praying for everyone, from kings on down, serves a dual purpose and is rooted in the fundamental doctrinal truth that "there is also one mediator between God and the human race, / Christ Jesus, himself human, / who gave himself as ransom for all" (2:5-6). First, it furthers God's purpose, for which Paul is appointed preacher and apostle, that everyone be saved and come to a knowledge of the truth. Emphasis on God's desire to save all people is as important for the contemporary reader of this letter as it was for the original readers in their situation. Nowhere in the New Testament is this desire more explicit than in 1 Timothy 2:4.

Second, it furthers the desire of the developing Christian community to have its members accepted as good citizens in civil society. The quiet, tranquil lives desired is described using a technical term, "devotion" (2:2), sometimes translated "religion." It is the word used in the Roman world for reverence for the gods and respect for traditional values and practices, a combination of piety and correct behavior. This much esteemed virtue receives little notice in the rest of the New Testament but is prominent in 1 Timothy and Titus (2:2; 3:16; 4:7, 8; 6:3, 5, 6, 11; Titus 1:1; 2:12). It is a virtue

to God our savior, ⁴who wills everyone to be saved and to come to knowledge of the truth.

⁵For there is one God.
There is also one mediator between
    God and the human race,
Christ Jesus, himself human,
⁶who gave himself as ransom for all.

This was the testimony at the proper time. ⁷For this I was appointed preacher and apostle (I am speaking the truth, I am not lying), teacher of the Gentiles in faith and truth.

⁸It is my wish, then, that in every place the men should pray, lifting up holy hands, without anger or argument. ⁹Similarly, [too,] women should adorn

that pertains to the special concern of 1 Timothy and Titus that Christians lead lives worthy of their calling, lives that can be held in high esteem by the surrounding world. This passage illustrates a developing understanding of the church, not as an isolated and dangerous sect but as a community that is open to all, and of Christian life as fully compatible with good citizenship.

2:8-15, 3:1a How men and women are to pray and live

In the introduction to this letter, Paul spoke of Timothy as "my true child in faith" (1:2), indicating an understanding of the church as a genuinely new family. Here and later in the letter (6:1-2, 17-19) there is a list of duties, often called a "household code." Such lists in other writings (Eph 5:22–6:9; Col 3:18–4:1; 1 Pet 2:13–3:8) focused on members of a familial household; here, however, the whole church, the household of God, is addressed.

The concern of these verses is with community worship that is filled with factions and quarreling. Men are addressed in 2:8 and simply told to pray "without anger or argument." The remainder of the chapter concerns women's behavior in the assembled community. Women are not only admonished about appropriate dress and conduct, but they are also forbidden "to teach or to have authority over a man" (2:12). It is not clear why women are singled out for such extensive treatment, but all three Pastoral Letters seem to accept the widespread belief at that time that women were notoriously unable to control their sexual passions (1 Tim 5:11-15; 2 Tim 3:6-7; Titus 2:4-5). The belief that women were weak-willed and easy prey to false teachers probably influenced the prohibition on public teaching and the requirement that they remain completely silent in the Christian assembly (2:11-12; 1 Cor 14:34-35). While some have suggested that the injunction to "be quiet" (2:12) refers not to prayer but to aggressive confrontations, this passage has provoked more discussion than any other in the Pastoral Letters in recent years. It must be acknowledged that great harm has come upon women throughout the history of the church because of understandings of this passage.

15

themselves with proper conduct, with modesty and self-control, not with braided hairstyles and gold ornaments, or pearls, or expensive clothes, [10]but rather, as befits women who profess reverence for God, with good deeds. [11]A woman must receive instruction silently and under complete control. [12]I do not permit a woman to teach or to have authority over a man. She must be quiet.

While women are in some ways subordinate to men in Paul's letters, one does find there women prophets (1 Cor 11:1-13) and a degree of equality among men and women (Gal 3:28). The unusual interpretation of the Adam and Eve story (Gen 2) used to support the subordination of women is likewise contrary to Paul's teaching, for Paul clearly speaks of Adam's sin, not Eve's (Rom 5:12-19). 1 Timothy's inventive interpretation of Genesis 2 (2:13-14) is, interestingly, a clear example of scriptural warrant for interpretive strategies that go beyond the original meaning of the text. One needs to go beyond the original meaning of 2:11-12 by reading this passage with a hermeneutic of suspicion. Hermeneutics involves the methods used to interpret a text. The apparent meaning of a text is often colored by cultural presuppositions that are now known to have been mistaken. A hermeneutics of suspicion is a method that questions the validity of these cultural presuppositions and seeks a deeper meaning in the text. This method enables contemporary readers to arrive at fresh meanings of the text that are free from the cultural assumptions of the past.

At the same time, one must recognize that just as past assumptions about family structures and power relationships were not absolute but rather culturally conditioned, the same can be said for what contemporary society regards as appropriate about family structures and power relationships. Reading the Pastoral Letters with a hermeneutic of suspicion can help contemporary readers go beyond the culturally conditioned values of both past and present centuries.

The message of this passage for the church of the first century as well as for the church today is that good order based on sound doctrine needs to be maintained in the church. Women throughout history have spoken powerfully for the kind of sound doctrine promoted by 1 Timothy. The church was blessed because St. Catherine of Sienna did not take the injunction to silence literally when she persuaded Pope Gregory XI to return from Avignon to Rome in 1376. She was clearly more interested in what is a primary concern of 1 Timothy, the preservation of authentic Christian tradition.

The final verse in the passage on women emphasizes the role of motherhood in the salvation of women (2:15). Childbearing, however, fits in with God's plan for salvation only when it is accompanied by faith and love, the

¹³For Adam was formed first, then Eve. ¹⁴Further, Adam was not deceived, but the woman was deceived and transgressed. ¹⁵But she will be saved through motherhood, provided women perse-

vere in faith and love and holiness, with self-control.

3 **Qualifications of Various Ministers.** ¹This saying is trustworthy: whoever aspires to the office of bishop ▸

---

hallmarks of Christian existence; by holiness, the condition of belonging to the Lord; and self-control, a quality valued in Hellenistic society and a continuing motif in 1 Timothy and Titus (2:9, 15; 3:2; Titus 1:8; 2:2, 5); qualities equally expected of women as well as of men. "This saying is trustworthy" (3:1a) pertains to what precedes rather than to what follows. This is the second use of this phrase in the Pastoral Letters, a phrase which usually signals a basic truth of early Christian faith (1 Tim 1:15; 4:9; 2 Tim 2:11; Titus 3:8). Like every other use of this phrase in the Pastoral Letters, it is connected with a statement on salvation. In this case it is used to ratify the previously expressed teaching on the salvation of Christian women and more broadly the teaching on salvation which began in 2:3-4 affirming that God "wills everyone to be saved and to come to knowledge of the truth" (2:4).

3:1b-7 Qualifications for bishops

After spelling out the duties of men and women in the community, the letter continues with listings of the qualifications for leadership positions in the community. The purpose of this passage is to provide a stable structure for the community in the face of forces that have the potential to cause its disintegration. The qualifications listed here, like the previous treatment of the role of women, are culturally conditioned and concerned with public respectability in the context of a particular culture. The only uniquely Christian features in these lists are the requirements that the bishop "not be a recent convert" (3:6) and that deacons hold "fast to the mystery of the faith with a clear conscience" (3:9).

The list contains no specification of the actual roles of bishops and deacons in the community, and apart from the two items mentioned above, the qualifications listed are typical of what would be expected of pagan and Jewish officials. All these qualifications, however, are in keeping with two major concerns of 1 Timothy and Titus, namely, that the community be well ordered under reliable leadership and that the Christian community, by reason of its integrity, be respected by the surrounding world (3:7). One qualification that appears in the lists for both bishop and deacon is that they not be lovers of money (3:3) or greedy for sordid gain (3:8). Leaders who are mercenary would clearly detract both from good order

desires a noble task. [2]Therefore, a bishop must be irreproachable, married only once, temperate, self-controlled, decent, hospitable, able to teach, [3]not a drunkard, not aggressive, but gentle, not contentious, not a lover of money. [4]He must manage his own household well, keeping his children under control with perfect dignity; [5]for if a man does not know how to manage his own household, how can he take care of the church of God? [6]He should not be a recent convert, so that he may not become conceited and thus incur the devil's punishment. [7]He must also have a good reputation among outsiders, so that he may not fall into disgrace, the devil's trap.

[8]Similarly, deacons must be dignified, not deceitful, not addicted to drink, not greedy for sordid gain, [9]holding fast to the mystery of the faith with a clear conscience. [10]Moreover, they should be tested first; then, if there is nothing against them, let them serve as deacons. [11]Women, similarly, should be dignified, not slanderers, but temperate and faithful in everything. [12]Deacons may be married only once and must manage their children and their households well. [13]Thus those who serve well as

within the community as well as from the reputation of the community in the surrounding world. This characteristic is specifically attributed to false teachers who are harming the community (6:5; see Titus 1:11).

It is tempting to see in the offices of bishop and deacon their well-defined positions as they appear in the developed church of the second century. Nevertheless, it is far from clear just how well defined these positions had become in the context of 1 Timothy and Titus. Another group that appears in these letters are the presbyters, who seem to be synonymous with bishops (5:17, 19; Titus 1:5-6). Timothy and Titus have significant administrative and teaching authority, and Titus himself is given the authority to appoint presbyters (Titus 1:5), but nowhere are Timothy and Titus called bishops. Whether bishops have the kind of authority described for Timothy and Titus is not clear.

3:8-13 Qualifications for deacons

How the office of deacon differs from that of bishop/presbyter is similarly unclear. The qualifications are similar, and the functions are not mentioned. The fact that they are listed second might indicate that here, just as in the later church, their role is subordinate to that of bishop. Even more problematic is the reference to women in verse 11. Some hold that this passage refers to deaconesses like Phoebe (Rom 16:1), but what her role was or what the role of these women were is not clear. It is possible that this verse refers not to deaconesses but to the wives of deacons, who, like their husbands, must have qualities that contribute to the good order of the community and its reputation in the surrounding world.

deacons gain good standing and much confidence in their faith in Christ Jesus.

The Mystery of Our Religion. [14]I am writing you about these matters, although I hope to visit you soon. [15]But if I should be delayed, you should know how to behave in the household of God, which is the church of the living God, the pillar and foundation of truth. [16]Undeniably great is the mystery of devotion,

> Who was manifested in the flesh,
> vindicated in the spirit,

3:14-15 Conclusion on the household of God

These verses bring to conclusion the first main section of the letter on the household of God (2:1–3:15) and serve as a transition to what follows. "These matters" (3:14) refers to all that has preceded in this section in the same way that "these things" (4:11) refers to all that precedes in each of the next two main sections of the letter. In this first main part of the letter Paul detailed Timothy's responsibilities for the household of God. While Timothy is temporarily in charge, Paul continues to be responsible for the community (1:11; 2:7) and plans to return (3:14). Paul's plans to visit his communities are often noted in his letters (Rom 15:24; 1 Cor 4:19; Phlm 22). Mention of these plans gives added importance to the letter, which is to take the place of Paul's authoritative presence, supporting 1 Timothy's intention of serving as a kind of church constitution for a developing Christian community. The good order that precedes and the opposition to false teaching that will follow are what Paul intends for the Christian community.

The Christian community is then described using two images, "the household of God" and "the church of the living God, the pillar and foundation of truth" (3:15). The first image treats the church as a well-ordered structure exhibiting proper behavior, the main concern of the passages that preceded. The second image focuses on the church as a living faith-community whose organization and moral life are based on the solid foundation of sound doctrine, the concern of the second main section of the letter.

SOUND DOCTRINE OF DEVOTION/RELIGION

I Tim 3:16–4:11

3:16 Mystery of devotion

The second main section of the letter begins by providing the theological basis for this solid foundation of truth by using what appears to be a passage from a liturgical hymn. The letter speaks of this solid foundation as "the mystery of devotion" (3:16), the second use of this technical term in this letter (see 2:2). The hymn sums up the content of Christian faith on which

seen by angels,
proclaimed to the Gentiles,
believed in throughout the world,
taken up in glory.

◄ **4** **False Asceticism.** ¹Now the Spirit explicitly says that in the last times

some will turn away from the faith by paying attention to deceitful spirits and demonic instructions ²through the hypocrisy of liars with branded consciences. ³They forbid marriage and require abstinence from foods that God created to be ►

Christian living is based. The use of passages from hymns or confessions is common in New Testament letters and serves to remind readers of the fundamental truths that they believe and express in their community worship. A similar passage from a hymn is used in 1 Peter 3:18-19, 22.

An indication that the passage in 1 Timothy is taken from a hymn is the fact that it consists of three balanced couplets: flesh-spirit (contrast), seen-proclaimed (complementary), world-glory (contrast). This passage summarizes the church's authentic faith in the paschal mystery: Jesus died on the cross (his manifestation in the flesh) and rose from the dead. He was first seen by angels then proclaimed by apostles to the Gentiles. People all over the world have come to believe in Jesus, who is now enthroned as Lord of the church and will come again to judge the living and the dead.

4:1-5 Problems in later times, apostasy

The letter here turns attention to the fundamental problem mentioned at the start of the letter—people teaching false doctrines (1:3), doctrines opposed to the fundamental truths of Christian faith just summarized in the hymn (3:16). False teachers, upsetting the lives of the faithful and dividing communities, had been a problem from the earliest days of Christianity. Paul dealt with false teachings in his early letters and communities. False teachers became especially troublesome as the church attempted to settle into a structured and sustainable existence.

So important is the matter of correct teaching that the author has raised the stakes from a simple contrast between truth and falsehood to an end-time contrast between the forces of good and the forces of evil (cf. 2 Tim 3:1-9). He appeals to the prophetic Spirit to set the stage for the end-time conflict, clearly the same Spirit who had vindicated the crucified Jesus in the preceding hymn (3:16). References to the Spirit are rare in the Pastoral Letters, with each reference emphasizing a different aspect of the Spirit (see 2 Tim 1:14; Titus 3:5). Here the prophetic Spirit foretells the end-time conflict with "deceitful spirits and demonic instructions" (4:1).

The notion that deceit is characteristic of the end times was common in the New Testament era. It is found in the Marcan apocalypse (Mark 13:5-6,

received with thanksgiving by those who believe and know the truth. ⁴For everything created by God is good, and nothing is to be rejected when received with thanksgiving, ⁵for it is made holy by the invocation of God in prayer.

Counsel to Timothy. ⁶If you will give these instructions to the brothers,

---

22) as well as in parallel passages in Matthew and Luke. False teachings are referred to elsewhere in the Pastoral Letters, but only here are specific issues identified, which are then refuted with an explicit argument. These two issues— "they forbid marriage and require abstinence from foods" (4:3)—are similar to problems Paul encountered at Corinth about marriage (1 Cor 7:1-3) and food (1 Cor 8:4-13; 10:23-33). The problem here might also be related to the claim by Hymenaeus (see 1 Tim 1:20) that the "resurrection has already taken place" (2 Tim 2:18). This claim is consistent with the teachings of a later heretical group, the Gnostics, who viewed the material world as evil. If those transformed by the saving grace of Jesus were already "resurrected," already living full spiritual lives, abstinence from physical pursuits such as sex, marriage, and food would be consistent with their denigration of the material world.

These errors are refuted by appealing, as Paul did (1 Cor 8:6; 10:26), to the one God who created all that is. "Everything created by God is good" (4:4) echoes the words of Genesis 1:31: "God looked at everything he had made, and he found it very good." The goodness of God's creation was tainted by sin, but the redemption won by Jesus has overcome all the evil caused by sin. Nevertheless, powerful sects preaching that the material world is evil have arisen throughout the history of the church. These included the Gnostics of the early church; the Manichees, among whom St. Augustine once was numbered; and the thirteenth-century Albigensians, against whom St. Dominic preached, to name but a few. According to 1 Timothy, everything created by God is not only good, but "it is made holy by the invocation of God in prayer" (4:5). This powerful assertion about the goodness of all that God creates is as important today as it has been throughout the history of Christianity. Receiving God's good creation in prayer pertains clearly to the common Christian practice of thanking God in prayer before meals, but it can pertain equally to the use of sex within marriage or to any other good thing.

4:6-10 Training for devotion, false versus true teachers

After reflecting on the conflicts of the end times (4:1-5), Paul addresses a charge to Timothy that involves a contrast between the true teacher exemplified in the person of Timothy and the false teachers discussed in 4:1-3. "These instructions" (4:6) probably refers to the previous instructions

you will be a good minister of Christ Jesus, nourished on the words of the faith and of the sound teaching you have followed. ⁷Avoid profane and silly myths. Train yourself for devotion, ⁸for, while physical training is of limited value, devotion is valuable in every respect, since it holds a promise of life both for the present and for the future. ⁹This saying is trustworthy and deserves full acceptance. ¹⁰For this we toil and struggle, because we have set our hope on the living God, who is the savior of all, especially of those who believe.

¹¹Command and teach these things. ¹²Let no one have contempt for your

---

on the goodness of creation. False teachers are concerned with "profane and silly myths" (4:7; see 1:4), while true teachers are concerned with "the words of the faith and of the sound teaching" (4:6). False teachers require unwarranted asceticism based on a false understanding of resurrection and the spiritual life (4:3). True teachers train for devotion (4:7), knowing that future life is still a promise (4:8, 10). Christians trained in devotion would lead lives that could be held in high esteem by the surrounding world. Training for devotion is somewhat like, but far more important than, physical training. "Devotion is valuable in every respect, since it holds a promise of life both for the present and for the future" (4:8).

This statement on the importance of devotion is the third of the trustworthy sayings to appear in the letter (see 1:15; 3:1). This saying is unique among the trustworthy sayings in the Pastoral Letters, since only here are specific implications of the saying spelled out. The first implication is "toil and struggle" (4:10). God has promised the life to come, but the path to that life will involve effort. There is, however, no suggestion here or elsewhere in this letter that the author is thinking of the kind of hardship and persecution that is discussed in 2 Timothy (2 Tim 3:10-12; 4:5). The second implication concerns Christian hope, an important theme in both this letter and in Titus (1 Tim 1:1; 4:10; 5:5; Titus 1:2; 2:13; 3:7). God is the ground and object of hope, which is fulfilled in the gift of eternal life. The final implication is God's gift of salvation. Every time a trustworthy saying appears in the Pastoral Letters it refers to some aspect of salvation. God wills that all people be saved, but God also wills that they come to a full knowledge of the truth (2:4). Those who do so are the faithful, whom God particularly wills to be saved. These are the ones who toil and struggle for devotion.

4:11 Conclusion

This second main section of the letter concludes with an instruction to "command and teach these things" (4:11; see 3:14; 6:2), a reference to all that has preceded in this section. Timothy is charged to command and

youth, but set an example for those who believe, in speech, conduct, love, faith, and purity. [13]Until I arrive, attend to the reading, exhortation, and teaching. [14]Do not neglect the gift you have, which was conferred on you through the prophetic word with the imposition of hands of the presbyterate. [15]Be diligent in these matters, be absorbed in them, so that your progress may be evident to

---

teach about training for devotion and the rejection of teaching that is opposed to the fundamentals of Christian faith.

INSTRUCTIONS ABOUT LEADERSHIP

1 Tim 4:12–6:2

4:12-16 Timothy's duties

After a discussion of true and false teachings, the third main section of the letter focuses on the duties of the leader of the community. In the previous verses Timothy was encouraged to "give these instructions" (4:6) and to "train yourself for devotion" (4:7). This section further expands on these two fundamental duties of a community leader. He is the church's authorized teacher and guardian of its faith, and he is to witness to that faith in the way he lives and performs his duties.

The overall concern of 1 Timothy and Titus for a stable Christian community with an authorized leadership is here manifest in the solemn description of Timothy's authorization for ministry: "through the prophetic word with the imposition of hands of the presbyterate" (4:14). This is the only passage in 1 Timothy dealing with how leaders assume their positions. It differs significantly from 2 Timothy, where Paul imposes hands on Timothy (2 Tim 1:6), transmitting his own authority. It differs as well from Titus, where Titus appoints presbyters (Titus 1:5). The intent of the present passages is to establish both the charismatic and the transmitted authority of the church leader. The charge "let no one have contempt for your youth" (4:12) is reminiscent of what Paul wrote about Timothy to the Corinthians: "no one should disdain him" (1 Cor 16:11). The narrative of the letter presumes that he is still a young man who has been raised up by the presbyterate to a position of leadership and enabled by the gift of the Spirit to "attend to the reading, exhortation, and teaching" (4:13).

The list of five qualities that Timothy is to model (4:12) are noteworthy, since they significantly differ from the list of six qualities in 2 Timothy that are observed in Paul (2 Tim 3:10-11). Common to both lists are faith and love, the hallmarks of Christian existence (see 1:14; 2:15; 6:11). 2 Timothy

everyone. [16]Attend to yourself and to your teaching; persevere in both tasks, for by doing so you will save both yourself and those who listen to you.

IV. Duties Toward Others

5 [1]Do not rebuke an older man, but appeal to him as a father. Treat younger men as brothers, [2]older women

---

also lists patience, endurance, persecutions, and sufferings, qualities important for the character and purpose of that letter. Instead of these, 1 Timothy lists speech, conduct, and purity, qualities more specific to the nature and purpose of 1 Timothy.

The passage concludes with a series of imperatives directed at Timothy: "be diligent . . . be absorbed . . . attend . . . persevere " (4:15-16), which emphasize the importance of his position and the seriousness of his responsibilities. He is to do these things for two reasons: first "so that your progress may be evident to everyone" (4:15). "Progress" is a technical term employed by Stoics and other philosophers, but appearing elsewhere in the New Testament only in Philippians 1:12, 25 (interestingly, the only book in the New Testament besides 1 Timothy that speaks of both bishops and deacons). "Progress" refers to a person's moral and spiritual evolution. For Plutarch, progress comes between natural dispositions and perfection. Virtues important in the surrounding world are important as well for 1 Timothy and Titus. Timothy's moral and religious development should not only inspire the Christian community but also bring credit to the community in the eyes of others. The second reason he is to do these things is to "save both yourself and those who listen to you" (4:16). God is the savior of all, but Timothy has been brought into this plan by reason of his authorization and spiritual gifts.

5:1-2 Respect for men and women, old and young

The instructions to Timothy continue, but the focus shifts from how he is to deal with false teaching to how he is to deal with the members of the household of God. The present section differs from earlier sections dealing with household members (2:8–3:13). There a household code (2:8-15) dealt with the behavior of various members of the community, followed by a section (3:1-13) dealing with qualifications and responsibilities for positions of leadership. The present section deals with how Timothy and others are to treat various members of the community, first considered in terms of age and sex. Greater attention is paid to older men, continuing an Old Testament concern for men in their old age (Sir 3:12-14), but all are to be treated with respect and kindness. Within the household of God, obligations toward one's immediate family are to be extended to all members of the community.

as mothers, and younger women as sisters with complete purity.

Rules for Widows. ³Honor widows who are truly widows. ⁴But if a widow has children or grandchildren, let these first learn to perform their religious duty to their own family and to make recompense to their parents, for this is pleasing to God. ⁵The real widow, who is all alone, has set her hope on God and continues in supplications and prayers night and day. ⁶But the one who is self-indulgent is dead while she lives. ⁷Command this, so that they may be irreproachable. ⁸And whoever does

not provide for relatives and especially family members has denied the faith and is worse than an unbeliever.

⁹Let a widow be enrolled if she is not less than sixty years old, married only once, ¹⁰with a reputation for good works, namely, that she has raised children, practiced hospitality, washed the feet of the holy ones, helped those in distress, involved herself in every good work. ¹¹But exclude younger widows, for when their sensuality estranges them from Christ, they want to marry ¹²and will incur condemnation for breaking their first pledge. ¹³And furthermore, they

5:3-16 Rules regarding widows

This long section addresses the place of widows in the community, obviously a matter of concern in the church at the time the letter was written. As with all members of the community, widows are to be treated with the respect that is owed them (5:3). There are, however, different categories of widows. First and foremost is "the real widow, who is all alone, has set her hope on God and continues in supplications and prayers night and day" (5:5). Christians have an obligation to provide for family members who become widows (5:4, 8, 16), but those left with no one to provide for them become the responsibility of the community. These real widows are to be "enrolled," a term which probably indicates not only that they are being provided for but also that they have some official role in the community. The qualifications laid down for being enrolled (5:9-10) are similar to qualifications listed for bishops and deacons (3:2-3, 8-9).

Besides these "real widows," there are the widows who have families that can provide for them, widows of any age who are self-indulgent (5:6), and younger widows, "less than sixty years old" (5:9), who might not be self-indulgent but might become so. The advice given about younger widows manifests concerns raised elsewhere in the Pastoral Letters. Women are especially prey to false teachers disturbing the church (2 Tim 3:6-7). Rather than risk succumbing either to the desire for marriage or to the wiles of false teachings (see Titus 1:11), it would be better for them to marry and manage a home and children (5:14). The recommendation to remarry should also be seen in connection with the false teachers' attack on marriage in 4:3. An

25

learn to be idlers, going about from house to house, and not only idlers but gossips and busybodies as well, talking about things that ought not to be mentioned. [14]So I would like younger widows to marry, have children, and manage a home, so as to give the adversary no pretext for maligning us. [15]For some have already turned away to follow Satan. [16]If any woman believer has widowed relatives, she must assist them; the church is not to be burdened, so that it will be able to help those who are truly widows.

Rules for Presbyters. [17]Presbyters who preside well deserve double honor, especially those who toil in preaching and teaching. [18]For the scripture says, "You shall not muzzle an ox when it is threshing," and, "A worker deserves his pay." [19]Do not accept an accusation against a presbyter unless it is supported

additional concern of these letters is the repute of the community in the surrounding world. Young widows should marry lest they fall into kinds of behavior that bring disrepute on the community (5:14).

5:17-22 Rules regarding presbyters

After dealing with those older widows who serve a special function within the community, the letter now deals with older men, presbyters, who have a special function in the community. It is not clear how the presbyters dealt with here are any different from the bishops of chapter 3. Titus 1:5-9 uses "bishop" and "presbyter" almost interchangeably, the term "presbyter" referring to the person's status within the community, a respected member of the community, and the term "bishop" referring to his function, exercising oversight and leadership in the community. Like Timothy, presbyters have a responsibility for teaching and preaching, what the qualifications for bishops state they must be able to do (3:2; Titus 1:9). Like widows, they are to be provided for by the community. In fact, presbyters "deserve double honor" (5:17). The scriptural basis provided in the next verse appears in two parts. The first is clearly from Deuteronomy 25:4 (see 1 Cor 9:9), but the second is a saying of Jesus (Matt 10:10; Luke 10:7). While some believe that only the first is referred to as Scripture, others feel that this passage may be early evidence for the conferral of scriptural status on New Testament literature or sources.

Just as there was a concern with widows who stray and bring disrepute on the community, there is an even greater concern with presbyters who sin. When accusations are brought against presbyters, they are entitled to what today would be called "due process." Those who indeed do sin, however, are to be reprimanded publicly, "so that the rest will also be afraid" (5:20). The need for harsh treatment of errant church leaders is all too evident in the contemporary church.

by two or three witnesses. ²⁰Reprimand publicly those who do sin, so that the rest also will be afraid. ²¹I charge you before God and Christ Jesus and the elect angels to keep these rules without prejudice, doing nothing out of favoritism. ²²Do not lay hands too readily on anyone, and do not share in another's sins. Keep yourself pure. ²³Stop drinking only water, but have a little wine for the sake of your stomach and your frequent illnesses.

²⁴Some people's sins are public, preceding them to judgment; but other people are followed by their sins. ²⁵Similarly, good works are also public; and even those that are not cannot remain hidden.

Rules for Slaves. ¹Those who are under the yoke of slavery must

---

The admonition that care should be taken not to "lay hands too readily on anyone" (5:22) could refer to the ordination of presbyters (see 4:14), but in the present context it more likely refers to the laying on of hands involved in the reconciliation of sinners. Timothy is exhorted not to play favorites but to reconcile to the community only those who have fully repented of their sins. The bottom line is a word of advice to Timothy, which applies, through him, to all with positions of leadership: "keep yourself pure" (5:22).

5:23-25 Timothy's duties
The final comment in verse 22, "keep yourself pure," connects as well to the verse that follows. Timothy bears a heavy responsibility for the church at Ephesus and must be both spiritually and physically fit for the task at hand. The rejection of a false dietary asceticism (4:3-4) is here reinforced by the recommendation to make proper use of the good things, like wine, created by God for one's physical well being (5:23). This advice to Timothy parallels the advice given earlier to young widows about remarriage (5:14), rejecting false teaching and extolling God's good creation. The emphasis on the public character of both sin and good deeds relates to the overall concern of 1 Timothy and Titus for the public perception of the Christian community. The behavior of Christian leaders, good or bad, will affect the public perception of the community. Whether or not their deeds are public, they will not long remain hidden.

6:1-2 Conclusion on slaves
In chapters 2 and 3 the letter had addressed the responsibilities and qualifications of various members of the community in the "household of God"—husbands and wives, bishops, and deacons. The previous chapter shifted the focus and looked at the way the community and its leaders should deal with certain members—older men, widows, and presbyters.

27

regard their masters as worthy of full respect, so that the name of God and our teaching may not suffer abuse. ²Those whose masters are believers must not take advantage of them because they are brothers but must give better service because those who will profit from their work are believers and are beloved. Teach and urge these things.

V. False Teaching and True Wealth

³Whoever teaches something different and does not agree with the sound words of our Lord Jesus Christ and the

---

Here the focus seems to shift back to the responsibilities of certain members within the community. Just as bishops and deacons are to conduct themselves in ways that bring honor to the Christian community, slaves are charged with a similar responsibility.

There is no suggestion here, nor generally in the New Testament, that the Christian community was to overthrow the social structures of society. In 1 Timothy and Titus especially, Christians are charged to behave as good citizens in what was considered a well-ordered society. Slaves are encouraged to fulfill their responsibilities to their masters, even to their Christian masters, "so that the name of God and our teaching may not suffer abuse" (6:1). The motive for similar advice to slaves in Titus is expressed positively: "so as to adorn the doctrine of God our savior in every way" (Titus 2:10).

Dealing with slaves at this point in the letter, shifting back to responsibilities of certain members of the community, is not really out of place. This third main section of the letter is concerned with the responsibilities of leaders in the community. Timothy is, as Paul describes himself in Titus 1:1, a slave of God, as are all those who exercise leadership roles. Timothy, above all, as a slave, must fulfill his responsibilities to his master. The final words of verse 2, "teach and urge these things" (cf. 3:14; 4:11), conclude this third main section of the letter. These words, which are unfortunately and inexplicably missing from many editions of the New American Bible, refer not just to the advice to slaves but to all the responsibilities that Timothy and other leaders, slaves of God, have been charged with in this section of the letter.

FALSE TEACHING AND TRUE WEALTH

I Tim 6:3-10, 17-19

6:3-10 The evils of false teaching exposed

The focus of the letter now shifts from the responsibilities of true teachers to a criticism of false teachers in this fourth and final main section of the letter. As in chapter 4, Timothy is advised to beware of false teachers and to be strong in adhering to correct doctrine, the doctrine that leads

religious teaching ⁴is conceited, understanding nothing, and has a morbid
disposition for arguments and verbal
disputes. From these come envy, rivalry, insults, evil suspicions, ⁵and mutual friction among people with
corrupted minds, who are deprived of
the truth, supposing religion to be a
means of gain. ⁶Indeed, religion with

contentment is a great gain. ⁷For we
brought nothing into the world, just as
we shall not be able to take anything out
of it. ⁸If we have food and clothing, we
shall be content with that. ⁹Those who
want to be rich are falling into tempta-
tion and into a trap and into many foolish and harmful desires, which plunge
them into ruin and destruction. ¹⁰For

to religion/devotion (6:3; see 2:2; 3:16; 4:7, 8; 5:4; 6:5, 6, 11). In this chapter
the correct understanding of religion is contrasted with the understanding of those who think that religion can be a source of material gain (6:5;
cf. Titus 1:11). These are the people who fall into erroneous beliefs and end
up experiencing a host of vices—"envy, rivalry, insults, evil suspicions,
and mutual friction" (6:4-5). They are the ones referred to earlier in the letter who have "turned to meaningless talk" (1:6) and are "paying attention
to deceitful spirits and demonic instructions through the hypocrisy of
liars with branded consciences" (4:1-2). "Religion with contentment" (6:6)
expressed the Stoic ideal of being content in any situation, but here it expresses a perspective on life restored by the saving mission of Christ. Religion is indeed a source of great gain if it leads to a Christian appreciation
for moderation and sufficiency. Those, however, who use religion to
achieve material wealth will stray into error and encounter an array of
evils, for "the love of money is the root of all evils" (6:10).

6:17-19 Conclusion on the wealthy

While this passage appears after the first part of the closing bracket
(6:11-16), it serves to conclude the fourth and final section of the body of
the letter on false teachers. This passage deals with a final group within
the household of God not yet treated in the letter—the rich. They are fittingly dealt with here and told not to be proud (6:17), after the emphasis
on the overarching power of God in the final doxology (6:15-16). While it
is wrong to use religion to pursue wealth, it is admirable to use wealth in
the service of religion, recognizing that the ultimate source of security is
not transient wealth but the eternal God. As with the earlier section on
slaves, this passage dealing with the wealthy is really not out of place,
since it concludes the previous section, which dealt with the connection of
false teaching and the inappropriate pursuit of wealth (6:5).

In a broader perspective, wealth is viewed in the same light as were
marriage and food. "Everything created by God is good, and nothing is to

the love of money is the root of all evils, and some people in their desire for it have strayed from the faith and have pierced themselves with many pains.

Exhortations to Timothy. ¹¹But you, man of God, avoid all this. Instead, pursue righteousness, devotion, faith, love, patience, and gentleness. ¹²Compete well for the faith. Lay hold of eternal life, to which you were called when you made the noble confession in the presence of many witnesses. ¹³I charge [you] before God, who gives life to all things, and before Christ Jesus, who

---

be rejected when received with thanksgiving" (4:4). Just as Timothy and all Christian leaders are slaves of God, they are to rely on God for all the good things they need to fulfill their ministries. The reason for the proper use of riches, like the reason for all the moral exhortations in this letter, is "to win the life that is true life" (6:19).

CLOSING BRACKET

I Tim 6:11-16, 20-21a

6:11-16 Timothy's responsibility and accountability

While the false teacher's misuse of religion leads to ruin, the true teacher's correct pursuit of religion leads to eternal life. This passage, together with 6:20-21a, closely parallels the opening bracket of the letter (1:12-20). That bracket appeared after the formal opening (1:1-2) and an expression of concern for the problem of false teachings (1:3-11). It began with a thanksgiving for the mercy and promise of eternal life extended to Paul, the true teacher (1:12-17).

In this final bracket Timothy is encouraged to follow the example of Paul, to "compete well for the faith" (6:12; see 1:18) and "to keep the commandment without stain or reproach" (6:14). His role of being a faithful witness parallels not only Paul's but also that of Jesus before Pilate (6:13). In the opening of the letter Timothy was addressed by Paul as "my true child in the faith" (1:2); here he is addressed as "man of God" (6:11), an expression used in the Old Testament for a person with a prophetic function (1 Sam 2:27; 1 Kgs 13:1). Its use recalls the prophetic charge to Timothy in the opening bracket (1:18).

Timothy is charged to keep "the commandment" (6:14), a term that appears nowhere else in the Pastoral Letters. In this context, however, it likely refers to the tasks entrusted to Timothy at the laying on of hands (4:14). It would involve both his teaching responsibilities as well as his responsibility to provide moral leadership by his own good example. He is to keep this commandment "until the appearance of our Lord Jesus

gave testimony under Pontius Pilate for the noble confession, ¹⁴to keep the commandment without stain or reproach until the appearance of our Lord Jesus Christ ¹⁵that the blessed and only ruler will make manifest at the proper time, the King of kings and Lord of lords, ¹⁶who alone has immortality, who dwells in unapproachable light, and whom no human being has seen or can see. To him be honor and eternal power. Amen.

Right Use of Wealth. ¹⁷Tell the rich in the present age not to be proud and not to rely on so uncertain a thing as wealth but rather on God, who richly provides us with all things for our enjoyment. ¹⁸Tell them to do good, to be rich in good works, to be generous, ready to share, ¹⁹thus accumulating as treasure a good foundation for the future, so as to win the life that is true life.

VI. Final Recommendation and Warning

²⁰O Timothy, guard what has been entrusted to you. Avoid profane babbling

---

Christ" (6:14), a reference to the eschatological parousia (second coming) of the risen Lord, similar to 1 Thessalonians 3:13; 5:23, but without suggesting that the appearance will occur during Timothy's lifetime.

This final charge to Timothy concludes with a doxology (6:15-16) that is strikingly similar to the doxology that concludes the thanksgiving in the opening bracket (1:17). Like that earlier doxology, it includes all four elements usually found in New Testament doxologies: the object of praise, "the King of kings and Lord of lords, who alone has immortality, who dwells in unapproachable light, and whom no human being has seen or can see"; an expression of praise, "honor and eternal power"; an indication of time, "eternal"; and a response, "Amen."

Unlike the doxology at 1:16 and unlike all the other New Testament passages that are commonly identified as doxologies, this one in chapter 6 is the only one that does not use the Greek word for "glory," *doxa*. Instead, this final doxology uses the word "power." While 1 Timothy and Titus respect the power of earthly rulers, their power is subject to God's, and only his is an "eternal power" (6:16).

6:20-21a Final recommendation

The final words of Hellenistic letters usually recapitulate and emphasize the main themes of the letter. The final words here complete the closing bracket by summarizing the advice given to Timothy throughout the letter, addressing Timothy directly, as in the opening bracket (1:18). They renew the warning about the dangerous opposition that threatens the faith (6:21; see 1:19-20). Timothy is to "guard what has been entrusted" (cf. 1:18) and "avoid profane babbling" (cf. 4:7).

31

and the absurdities of so-called knowledge. ²¹By professing it, some people

have deviated from the faith.
Grace be with all of you.

BLESSING

1 Tim 6:21b

This letter's closing is, curiously, the shortest of all such closings in the New Testament. Both 2 Timothy and Titus, like Paul's authentic letters, include second- and third-person greetings as well as references to travel plans prior to the final blessing. These omissions serve only to reinforce the focus of this letter on the singular responsibility of Timothy, the community leader, to overcome opposition by adhering to sound doctrine in promoting the internal life of the community as well as in securing its good reputation in the surrounding world. The blessing itself, "grace be with all of you," is identical to that found at the end of 2 Timothy. Titus and most of Paul's letters have longer blessings, but all, except Romans, use the identical words found in 1 Timothy. In all these letters, including Philemon, the blessing is addressed to "you" in the plural, an indication that even those letters addressed to individuals were intended to be heard by the larger community.

The Second Letter to Timothy

Of the three Pastoral Letters, 2 Timothy contains by far the greatest amount of biographical material about Paul. Most agree that it contains material dating from Paul, and some feel that it was written by Paul himself. It was probably the first of the Pastoral Letters to be written, possibly by someone other than the author of 1 Timothy and Titus. One of the most noticeable differences between 2 Timothy and the other Pastoral Letters is the large number of references to persons and places, but there are other, more significant differences. Unlike these other letters, 2 Timothy has no codes of behavior for community members, no discussion of qualifications for various ministries, and no element of anti-Jewish polemic.

2 Timothy is essentially a reflection on the ministry of Paul and on how that ministry is to be continued after his death. Timothy is the person closely associated with Paul's ministry and has become his designated successor. The two focuses of this letter, Paul and Timothy, highlight the succession of the latter in the ministry of the former. Though there is mention of Timothy's responsibility to instruct others who will in turn become teachers (2:2), the letter is mainly concerned with Timothy's own vocation and ministry. Fidelity to his vocation demands that he follow the sound teaching he learned from Paul. Timothy is to be loyal to his faith and not ashamed of bearing witness either to the Lord or to Paul. The letter's emphasis on suffering contrasts with the goal in 1 Timothy and Titus of leading quiet and peaceable lives in society.

In 2 Timothy Paul is presented as imprisoned and in chains, deserted by others because of the shame brought on by his chains. Paul is nonetheless confident of the salvific effects of his prolonged imprisonment and proclaims Christ as sovereign judge over all. Paul's fearlessness in the face of evil is the basis of the advice to Timothy to protect his community from the impact of false teaching (2:14–3:9) without fearing the personal attacks that may result (3:10-12). Paul is presented as the model for Timothy in both word (1:13; 2:2; 3:14) and deed (3:10-11). There is no suggestion, however, that Timothy should be a model, as in the other Pastoral Letters, where Timothy and Titus are to serve as models for the communities they lead (see 1 Tim 4:12-15; Titus 2:7-8). The advice in 2 Timothy focuses primarily on Timothy. Not only are there no specific directions concerning the community, but there is no indication of where Timothy is presumably located. While 1:18 might be read as a hint that the community he is leading is Ephesus, 4:12 indicates that although he may once have been there, he no longer is.

While 1 Timothy and Titus are concerned with the organization of the church in the post-Pauline era and were probably written later than 2 Timothy, both presume that Paul is still active and free to travel. Since 2 Timothy is chronologically located near the end of Paul's life, its position after 1 Timothy seems natural. This letter reads like Paul's last will and testament, containing the parting advice of one convinced that his present imprisonment will end with his death. While addressed to Timothy, it speaks powerfully to a modern culture that needs to regain its focus on the value of loyalty, fidelity, and suffering for the sake of the gospel.

The Second Letter to Timothy

I. Address

1 **Greeting.** ¹Paul, an apostle of Christ Jesus by the will of God for the promise of life in Christ Jesus, ²to Timothy, my dear child: grace, mercy, and peace from God the Father and Christ Jesus our Lord.

Thanksgiving. ³I am grateful to God, ▶ whom I worship with a clear conscience

---

1:1-2 The opening

The letter opens, as is typical of Hellenistic letters, with the identification of both the sender and the receiver, followed by a greeting. The sender, Paul, is identified as "an apostle of Christ Jesus by the will of God for the promise of life in Christ Jesus." The first part, "an apostle of Christ Jesus by the will of God," is identical to the identification at 2 Corinthians 1:1 (cf. 1 Cor 1:1). This identification echoes Paul's conviction that the will of God determined the shape of his life and his work as an apostle. The identification in this letter, however, continues by focusing on "the promise of life" as the purpose of Paul's apostolate. The phrase "promise of life" is an expression used only in the Pastoral Letters (cf. 1 Tim 4:8). God has promised and guarantees the gift of eternal life. Just as the hope of eternal life motivated the apostolate of Paul, this hope should motivate Timothy and the readers of this letter.

Timothy, the receiver of the letter, is identified as "my dear child." In 1 Timothy he is called "my true child in faith" (1 Tim 1:2), similar to what Titus is called, "my true child in our common faith" (Titus 1:4). "True child" suits the purpose of these letters as mandates to Timothy and Titus to minister in Paul's name. "Dear child" in 2 Timothy uses the language denoting deep friendship that Paul had used of Timothy (1 Cor 4:17). Its use in 2 Timothy suits the purpose of the letter as a reflection on Paul's ministry in the context of a personal farewell and a designation of Timothy as the legitimate and faithful heir who will carry on the Pauline legacy.

▶ This symbol indicates a cross reference number in the *Catechism of the Catholic Church*. See page 79 for number citations.

as my ancestors did, as I remember you constantly in my prayers, night and day. ⁴I yearn to see you again, recalling your tears, so that I may be filled with joy, ⁵as I recall your sincere faith that first lived in your grandmother Lois and in your mother Eunice and that I am confident lives also in you.

II. Exhortations to Timothy

The Gifts Timothy Has Received.
⁶For this reason, I remind you to stir into flame the gift of God that you have through the imposition of my hands. ⁷For God did not give us a spirit of cowardice but rather of power and love and self-control. ⁸So do not be ashamed

---

The opening concludes with the greeting typical of all Paul's letters, but with the addition of "mercy" to the typical Pauline "grace and peace." Both 1 and 2 Timothy add this word to the greeting, but not Titus.

1:3-5 Thanksgiving

Pauline letters typically have a passage immediately after the opening in which Paul gives thanks to God for what God has done for the community or person to whom the letter is addressed. These thanksgivings also serve to summarize the main themes of the letter. 2 Timothy, alone among the Pastoral Letters, has this characteristic Pauline thanksgiving. While 1 Timothy has a kind of belated thanksgiving (1 Tim 1:12-17), it is different in form and function from the typical Pauline thanksgiving. The thanksgiving in 2 Timothy is more typical, although the words used, *echō charin* (cf. 1 Tim 1:12), are different from the Pauline *eucharistō* (Rom 1:8; 1 Cor 1:4; Phil 1:3; 1 Thess 1:2; Phlm 4).

This thanksgiving stresses the double focus of the letter, Paul and Timothy, by thanking God for Timothy's faith (1:5) and expressing Paul's desire to see Timothy once more (1:4). Paul's desire to see Timothy actually frames and colors the entire letter. In the final chapter Timothy is urged to come quickly and to bring Mark (4:9, 11, 21). Timothy, the other focus of the letter, is presented as one in whom the true faith lives on, though the emphasis on faith and the desire for the visit suggests that Timothy's faith may have been a matter of concern.

TIMOTHY'S VOCATION AND PAUL'S SUFFERING

2 Tim 1:6-18

1:6-14 Pauline model of vocation

The dual focus of this letter is evident in the sequencing of four exhortations to Timothy to carry on Paul's ministry (1:6-14; 2:1-7; 2:14-26; 3:10-17). These exhortations are separated by doctrinal material and sections dealing

Ruins of an early Christian basilica at Ephesus in Asia Minor

of your testimony to our Lord, nor of me, a prisoner for his sake; but bear your share of hardship for the gospel with the strength that comes from God.

⁹He saved us and called us to a holy life, not according to our works but according to his own design and the grace bestowed on us in Christ Jesus before time began, ¹⁰but now made manifest through the appearance of our savior Christ Jesus, who destroyed death and brought life and immortality to light through the gospel, ¹¹for which I was appointed preacher and apostle and teacher. ¹²On this account I am suffering these things; but I am not ashamed, for

---

with Paul's life and imminent departure. This first exhortation deals with Timothy's vocation, which flows from and is modeled on Paul's. An interesting feature of this exhortation is the frequent use of the first person plural pronoun. Paul and Timothy are viewed together, especially in the center of this chiastically arranged exhortation (1:9-10) as saved and called to their vocations by the saving grace of Christ's death and resurrection.

The exhortation begins and ends by speaking of their common vocation as based on the gift of the Spirit, a gift that is transmitted from Paul to Timothy (1:6-7, 13-14). Just before the center Paul encourages Timothy to bear the hardships of his ministry, not being ashamed either of his testimony to his crucified Lord or of Paul, now a chained prisoner (1:8). Right after the center Paul notes how he has suffered for his ministry, not being ashamed either of his sufferings or of his Lord (1:11-12). In 2 Timothy and in the undisputed letters, but not in 1 Timothy or Titus, suffering is integral to Paul's self-understanding (Rom 8:35-39; 1 Cor 4:9-13; 2 Cor 4:7-11; Gal 6:14-17; Phil 3:8-11; 1 Thess 2:2).

The exhortation opens with a reference to the transmission of office from Paul to Timothy "through the imposition of my hands" (1:6), a transmission that involved the gift of the Spirit. The term used here, *charisma*, was coined by Paul to distinguish real gifts of the Spirit from ecstatic phenomena, *pneumatika* (see 1 Cor 12:1, 4). It is a term used in the New Testament only in the letters of Paul and in the literature dependent on him, a term that highlights the gratuitous nature of the gifts and points to their ecclesial function. Everywhere in Paul and in the Pastoral Letters the gift of the Spirit is for building up the church as the body of Christ.

A similar passage in 1 Timothy speaks of Timothy's gift being conferred through the imposition of hands of the presbyterate (1 Tim 4:14). In 2 Timothy it is Paul alone who imposes hands. Both passages refer to the practice attested to elsewhere in the New Testament and the early church of using the imposition of hands for the transference of power, the appointment to office, and the conferral of the gift of the Spirit.

I know him in whom I have believed and am confident that he is able to guard what has been entrusted to me until that day. [13]Take as your norm the sound words that you heard from me, in the faith and love that are in Christ Jesus. ▶

The differences between the passages illustrate the differences between these two letters. 1 Timothy is concerned with the community as a whole and shows Timothy being brought into the ministry by a group of elders to share in their responsibility for leading an orderly Christian community. 2 Timothy is concerned with the specific role of the departing Paul in designating Timothy as his successor, who, like him, will be expected to accept his share of hardship for the gospel. The advice in verse 8 flows from the previous verses. Because of the strength that comes from God's gift of the Spirit transmitted by Paul, Timothy can endure the hardships involved in testifying to the Lord, not being ashamed either of the Lord or of Paul.

The hymn-like central section of this exhortation (1:9-10) attributes three qualities to God's saving purpose. First, it is gratuitous. Like Paul in the letter to the Romans, this letter establishes a clear contrast between human works and divine grace. Second, it is accomplished in Christ Jesus, and third, the initiative derives from all eternity. Even though this salvation was made manifest in the saving work of Jesus Christ, it was willed by God from all eternity. This brief passage is an interesting condensation of the theology, Christology, and eschatology of the Pastoral Letters. The one God establishes his purpose for salvation from all eternity. That salvation is made manifest by Christ's "appearance," which here refers to the past appearance of the Savior Christ Jesus, who destroyed death and brought life and immortality. Later in the letter the eschatological picture will be completed when the same term "appearance" is used to refer to a future appearance of Christ Jesus, who is to judge the living and the dead (4:8; cf. 1 Tim 6:14; Titus 2:13). Christian life, for the Pastoral Letters, lies between these two appearances of Christ Jesus.

This life is now available through the gospel for which Paul "was appointed preacher and apostle and teacher" (1:11). As he hands on his ministry to Timothy, Paul expresses confidence that Christ Jesus is able to guard what has been entrusted to Paul "until that day" (1:12), a clear reference to the final day when Christ will be revealed as God's eschatological agent (cf. 1:18; 4:8). The exhortation concludes with the mandate to Timothy to "guard this rich trust with the help of the holy Spirit" (1:14). The confidence that Christ will guard this trust between his two appearances

¹⁴Guard this rich trust with the help of the holy Spirit that dwells within us.

Paul's Suffering. ¹⁵You know that everyone in Asia deserted me, including Phygelus and Hermogenes. ¹⁶May the Lord grant mercy to the family of Onesiphorus because he often gave me new heart and was not ashamed of my chains. ¹⁷But when he came to Rome, he promptly searched for me and found me. ¹⁸May the Lord grant him to find mercy from the Lord on that day. And you know very well the services he rendered in Ephesus.

is based on the belief that Timothy and those who follow him will be aided by the holy Spirit in transmitting the true gospel of Jesus Christ. Here 2 Timothy expresses the distinctively Pauline idea of the indwelling of the holy Spirit (1 Cor 3:16; 6:19) more clearly than do the isolated references to the Spirit in the other Pastoral Letters (1 Tim 4:1; Titus 3:5).

1:15-18 False and faithful friends

This passage is the first of several biographical passages in this letter. Together with the last such passage, 4:16-18, it speaks of Paul's being without human contact, a lonely prisoner about to die. These two passages, just after the beginning and just before the end, share in the framing function of the appeals for Timothy to visit Paul (1:4; 4:9, 11, 21) and help define the letter as a testamentary farewell. The mention of Onesiphorus in both passages contributes to their framing function. Ephesus (1:18) in Asia (1:15) was where Paul exercised much of his apostolate and where he left a thriving Christian community. Ephesus was also where almost everyone abandoned him on his arrest. Now in Rome he draws on this experience to encourage Timothy, who once was in Ephesus but probably no longer is there (see 4:12). Onesiphorus, who alone was not ashamed of Paul's chains, can serve as a model for Timothy not to be ashamed either of Paul or of his "testimony to our Lord" (1:8).

This passage contains two prayers for mercy—one for the family of Onesiphorus (1:16), the other for Onesiphorus himself (1:18). These prayers for mercy recall the note in Philippians that God had shown mercy to Epaphroditus because of his service to Paul (Phil 2:25-27). They also relate to the addition of "mercy" to the greeting at 1:2. The first prayer was for mercy in the present, but the second is for mercy in the eschatological future, "that day," which Paul had spoken about in reference to himself (1:12). The second prayer might imply that Onesiphorus is already dead, in which case it would be one of the earliest examples of Christian prayer for the dead.

2 **Timothy's Conduct.** ¹So you, my child, be strong in the grace that is in Christ Jesus. ²And what you heard from me through many witnesses entrust to faithful people who will have the ability to teach others as well. ³Bear your share of hardship along with me like a good soldier of Christ Jesus. ⁴To

---

EXHORTATION TO BE STRONG
AND ENDURE SUFFERING

2 Tim 2:1-13

2:1-7 The hardships of faithful ministry

Like the first exhortation, this second exhortation begins and ends with a reference to what the Lord has given to Timothy (1:6, 14; 2:1, 7). However, while the first exhortation focused on the gift of God through the holy Spirit, this exhortation emphasizes the task that has been entrusted to Timothy. Timothy, with "the grace that is in Christ Jesus" (2:1), is to entrust to others what he has learned from Paul. These others, in turn, will be able to continue the chain of faithful transmission.

Significantly, 2 Timothy uses a technical term for "entrust" that in ancient times was used to refer to some kind of treasure, such as a valuable item or a sacred story, that was entrusted to another. This sacred trust, the gospel of salvation, is referred to three times in this letter as that with which Paul has been entrusted (1:12), that which Timothy is to guard with the help of the holy Spirit (1:14), and finally that which Timothy is to hand on to others who will continue its transmission (2:2). This term is used only once in the other Pastoral Letters, in the conclusion to 1 Timothy, where Timothy is urged to "guard what has been entrusted to you" (1 Tim 6:20).

These other letters use different language to speak of that with which Paul has been entrusted (1 Tim 1:11; Titus 1:3) and what Paul entrusts to Timothy (1 Tim 1:18), but they never speak of Timothy or Titus entrusting it to others. While Titus is to appoint leaders for orderly community life (Titus 1:5), the transmission of Paul's gospel to future evangelists is a concern only of 2 Timothy. Timothy is not alone in passing on Paul's teaching. There were "many witnesses" (2:2), but clearly not all of them remained faithful witnesses. Timothy's task is to establish a chain of transmission involving faithful witnesses, a task that will involve hardships like those Paul is enduring (cf. 1:12).

The hardships to be endured are compared to the hard work associated with soldiers, athletes, and farmers. Athletes compete to achieve "the

satisfy the one who recruited him, a soldier does not become entangled in the business affairs of life. ⁵Similarly, an athlete cannot receive the winner's crown except by competing according to the rules. ⁶The hardworking farmer ought to have the first share of the crop. ⁷Reflect on what I am saying, for the Lord will give you understanding in everything.

⁸Remember Jesus Christ, raised from the dead, a descendant of David: such is my gospel, ⁹for which I am suffering, even to the point of chains, like a criminal. But the word of God is not chained. ¹⁰Therefore, I bear with everything for the sake of those who are chosen, so that they too may obtain the salvation that is in Christ Jesus, together with eternal glory. ¹¹This saying is trustworthy:

---

winner's crown" (2:5). If Timothy bears the hardships of his ministry "like a good soldier of Christ Jesus" (2:3), he is assured that the Lord will give him the understanding needed to fulfill the task of faithful transmission (2:7). While 1 Timothy uses the athletic image in discussing training for devotion (1 Tim 4:7-8) and metaphors of competition (1 Tim 1:18; 6:12), neither 1 Timothy nor Titus suggests that Christian life will involve suffering. In both these letters advice is given to be under the control of authorities (Titus 3:1) and to pray for kings that "we may lead a quiet and tranquil life" (1 Tim 2:2). 2 Timothy alone among the Pastorals links fidelity to the gospel to a life that will involve hardship and suffering. Here Paul's suffering is presented as the model for Timothy (2:3, 8-9; cf. 3:12).

2:8-13 The gospel and its reward

The letter next identifies the message to be transmitted: the gospel for which Paul is suffering, "Jesus Christ, raised from the dead, a descendant of David" (2:8). Being introduced with "remember," these words are clearly an early creedal formulation that uses terminology employed in Paul's letters. "Raised from the dead" is language Paul commonly uses to refer to the resurrection. In Romans 1:3 Paul uses the phrase "descended from David" to identify Jesus as the Messiah, the expected ideal king of Israel. These expressions are not used elsewhere in the Pastoral Letters. They are used here to recall the traditional faith of the church with which Timothy has been entrusted. Paul is suffering in chains for these words, but the words are not chained. Timothy's task is to continue the transmission of these words so that others may "obtain the salvation that is in Christ Jesus."

This passage concludes with another selection of traditional material, probably a section of a hymn, assuring Timothy and the readers of the letter that fidelity with Christ means victory with the Lord (2:11-13). It is

If we have died with him
  we shall also live with him;
¹²if we persevere
  we shall also reign with him.
But if we deny him
  he will deny us.
¹³If we are unfaithful
  he remains faithful,
  for he cannot deny himself.

**III. Instructions Concerning
False Teaching**

Warning against Useless Disputes.
¹⁴Remind people of these things and charge them before God to stop disputing about words. This serves no useful purpose since it harms those who listen. ¹⁵Be eager to present yourself as ac-

---

introduced by "this saying is trustworthy," a phrase regularly used in the Pastoral Letters to introduce a basic truth of early Christian faith (1 Tim 1:15; 3:1; 4:9; Titus 3:8). The four-line selection opens with the Pauline notion that Christian life can be spoken of as dying with Christ (cf. Rom 6:3; Gal 2:19-20). The four lines from this hymn have a recurring pattern that would lead one to expect the final phrase to be "he will be unfaithful." Surprisingly, it is instead "he remains faithful, / for he cannot deny himself" (2:13).

Paul often affirms the absolute fidelity of God (see 1 Cor 1:9). Here the absolute fidelity of God is attributed to Christ Jesus. This section, whose purpose is to exhort Timothy to be strong and endure hardships for the gospel, concludes with an assurance of the absolute fidelity of Christ. While the immediate concern of this passage is with the responsibilities of a first-century evangelist, its message applies equally well to people living out their Christian vocation in any way in any age. Jesus, the Savior and Judge, remains true to his people regardless of how faithful they may or may not be.

DANGER OF FALSE TEACHING

2 Tim 2:14–3:9

2:14-26 Dealing with false teachers

The first exhortation to Timothy focused on the gift of God through the holy Spirit (1:6-14), and the second on the task entrusted to Timothy (2:1-7). This third exhortation deals with how he is to fulfill the charge to entrust to faithful people what he has heard from Paul in light of the ever-present danger of false teaching. The danger arises because people dispute about words (2:14), quarrel because of foolish and ignorant debates (2:23), and become more and more godless as a result of profane and idle talk (2:16).

ceptable to God, a workman who causes no disgrace, imparting the word of truth without deviation. ¹⁶Avoid profane, idle talk, for such people will become more and more godless, ¹⁷and their teaching will spread like gangrene. Among them are Hymenaeus and Philetus, ¹⁸who have deviated from the truth by saying that [the] resurrection has already taken place and are upsetting the faith of some. ¹⁹Nevertheless, God's solid foundation stands, bearing this inscription, "The Lord knows those who are his"; and, "Let everyone who calls upon the name of the Lord avoid evil."

²⁰In a large household there are vessels not only of gold and silver but also of wood and clay, some for lofty and others for humble use. ²¹If anyone cleanses himself of these things, he will be a vessel for lofty use, dedicated, beneficial to the master of the house, ready for every good work. ²²So turn ▶

Paul's advice to Timothy for dealing with this problem is twofold. First, he must be pure in himself. "Turn from youthful desires and pursue righteousness, faith, love, and peace, along with those who call on the Lord with purity of heart" (2:22). If he can present himself "as acceptable to God, a workman who causes no disgrace" (2:15), he will be able to impart "the word of truth without deviation" (2:15). Second, he must himself "avoid foolish and ignorant debates" (2:23) and then be able to charge others to stop engaging in useless disputes.

The basis for this advice is found in the center of this passage, where Old Testament texts are cited as "God's solid foundation" (2:19). "The Lord knows those who are his" is quoted from Numbers 16:5, where it dealt with a revolt against Moses. God will protect and empower those who are doing his work, not the false teachers. The second quote is even more important. "Let everyone who calls upon the name of the Lord avoid evil" (2:19) is a combination of allusions to Isaiah 26:13 and Sirach 17:21. God calls whom he wills, but humans must accept the call by themselves calling "on the Lord with purity of heart" (2:22) and avoiding the kind of behavior that is harmful to the gospel. The next chapter has the familiar verse on the inspiration and usefulness of Scripture (3:16-17), but the passage in 2:19 is the only Old Testament passage actually cited in this letter. The following two verses (2:20-21) clearly anticipate the passage in 3:16-17. Timothy and others entrusted with Paul's gospel are compared to various kinds of vessels that, when cleansed, become vessels "for lofty use, dedicated, beneficial to the master of the house, ready for every good work" (2:21).

The next verse encapsulates an aspect of this letter that has timeless significance for Christians—the essential link between Christian faith and

from youthful desires and pursue righteousness, faith, love, and peace, along with those who call on the Lord with purity of heart. ²³Avoid foolish and ignorant debates, for you know that they breed quarrels. ²⁴A slave of the Lord should not quarrel, but should be gentle with everyone, able to teach, tolerant, ²⁵correcting opponents with kindness. It may be that God will grant them repentance that leads to knowledge of the truth, ²⁶and that they may return to their senses out of the devil's snare, where they are entrapped by him, for his will.

3 **The Dangers of the Last Days.** ¹But understand this: there will be terrifying times in the last days. ²People

---

the life of virtue. Timothy and all Christians can and should lead lives of exemplary virtue precisely because they have called "on the Lord with purity of heart" (2:22). For Christians, their pattern of behavior is an expression of their deepest convictions.

While this exhortation is primarily concerned with Timothy and others entrusted with Paul's gospel, it does shed some light on the false teachers. Just before the center of this passage, two of them, Hymenaeus and Philetus, are identified, as well as their false teaching "that [the] resurrection has already taken place" (2:18). While specific moral issues appear elsewhere (see 1 Tim 4:3), this is the only precise false doctrine identified in any of the Pastoral Letters. Hymenaeus and Alexander (cf. 4:14) were identified as enemies of Paul in 1 Timothy 1:20, although their errors were not mentioned there.

Paul had taught that in baptism we die and rise with Christ (Rom 6:8; cf. 2 Cor 6:14-15). Some in Corinth had distorted Paul's teaching by denying the future resurrection of the dead (1 Cor 15:12), probably maintaining what was being taught by Hymenaeus and Philetus, that is, that Christians already enjoyed the fullness of resurrected life. Paul, as well as the Pastoral Letters, clearly teaches that although we have died with Christ and now live with him, there will be a future resurrection when all will be judged on the life they have led (Rom 14:10, 12; 1 Tim 6:12-16; 2 Tim 4:1, 8).

The exhortation concludes with advice on dealing with false teachers, correcting them with kindness so that "they may return to their senses out of the devil's snare" (2:26), advice that sounds less harsh than what Paul is said to have done in 1 Timothy, handing them "over to Satan to be taught not to blaspheme" (1 Tim 1:20; cf. Titus 3:10-11).

3:1-9 False teaching in the last days

In the previous exhortation Timothy was urged to "pursue righteousness, faith, love, and peace, along with those who call on the Lord with

will be self-centered and lovers of money, proud, haughty, abusive, disobedient to their parents, ungrateful, irreligious, ³callous, implacable, slanderous, licentious, brutal, hating what is good, ⁴traitors, reckless, conceited, lovers of pleasure rather than lovers of God, ⁵as they make a pretense of religion but deny its power. Reject them. ⁶For some of these slip into homes and make captives of women weighed down by sins, led by various desires, ⁷always trying to learn but never able to reach a knowledge of the truth. ⁸Just as Jannes and Jambres opposed Moses, so they also oppose the truth—people of depraved mind, unqualified in the faith. ⁹But they will not make further progress, for their foolishness will be plain to all, as it was with those two.

---

purity of heart" (2:22), in contrast to false teachers who taught that the resurrection had already occurred. Here the contrast is intensified by advancing the context to the last days (cf. 1 Tim 4:1-5). The last days are distinguished from "that day" (1:18; 4:8), the day when the Lord will appear as just judge. The last days precede "that day." They will be dangerous times; the church will be beset by people who will harm the faithful with cruelty, violence, and aggressiveness. Here, as elsewhere in the Pastoral Letters, false teaching leads to base morality, just as good teaching leads to good morality. False teaching can be easily recognized as such by the results it produces.

The virtue of religion/devotion, prominently treated in 1 Timothy (1 Tim 2:2; 3:16; 4:7, 8; 6:3, 5, 6, 11), is here mentioned in terms of its false understanding: "they make a pretense of religion but deny its power" (3:5). In 1 Timothy it was observed that some think religion can be a source of material gain. These are people who fall into erroneous beliefs and end up experiencing a host of vices: "envy, rivalry, insults, evil suspicions, and mutual friction" (1 Tim 6:4-5). In 2 Timothy the list is longer and the evils more intense (3:2-4).

The danger posed by false teachers is further illustrated by the evil influence they are able to exert on impressionable women. These women, eager to learn but lacking the erudition to distinguish true from false teaching, are led by their passions to accept appealing but perverse teachings (3:6-7). All three Pastoral Letters seem to accept the widespread belief at that time that women were notoriously unable to control their sexual passions (1 Tim 5:11-15; Titus 2:4-5). The false teachers who impress women are compared to the Egyptian magicians who were clever enough to impress Pharaoh but opposed the truth that came from God (3:8-9). They turned their staffs into snakes, as had Aaron, but Aaron's staff swallowed their staffs (Exod 7:11-12).

Paul's Example and Teaching. ¹⁰You have followed my teaching, way of life, purpose, faith, patience, love, endurance, ¹¹persecutions, and sufferings, such as happened to me in Antioch, Iconium, and Lystra, persecutions that I endured. Yet from all these things the Lord delivered me. ¹²In fact, all who want to live religiously in Christ Jesus will be persecuted. ¹³But wicked people and charlatans will go from bad to worse, deceivers and deceived. ¹⁴But you, remain faithful to what you have learned and believed, because you know from

---

PAUL'S EXAMPLE AND TIMOTHY'S COMMISSION

2 Tim 3:10–4:8

3:10-17 Imitation of Paul and the role of Scripture

The previous description of intensified evil in the end times sets the stage for this fourth and final exhortation to Timothy. With the approach of the end times, wicked people will become even more so (3:13) and good people will be persecuted (3:12). Interestingly, the term used to describe the good people who will be persecuted is the same term, "religion/devotion," which in 1 Timothy and Titus is that all-important virtue that will secure respect for the Christian community in the surrounding world.

Timothy is reminded about what he knows of Paul and is encouraged to remain faithful in following him (3:14). Timothy is reminded of nine important aspects of Paul's heritage that he is to follow (3:10-11). First among these is his teaching, the subject of much of this letter (1:13-14; 2:2, 8-9). Timothy is also aware of Paul's way of life and purpose. Timothy is aware as well of the six qualities that characterized Paul's life: the Christian virtues of faith, patience, love, and endurance (3:10), which were the basis of his teaching, life, and purpose, and the persecutions and suffering (3:11) that were the inevitable result. Just as Paul had responded to God's call to work as an apostle, so too should Timothy. In the Acts of the Apostles Paul is said to have visited the three cities mentioned here—Antioch, Iconium, and Lystra (Acts 13:1–14:23)—and to have commented, "It is necessary for us to undergo many hardships to enter the kingdom of God" (Acts 14:22). It is interesting to note that Timothy came from one of these cities, Lystra, born of a Jewish mother who became a believer, and a Greek father (Acts 16:1).

Timothy's faith, a faith that he received from his mother and grandmother, was mentioned in the first chapter (1:5). Presumably it was from them that he first learned the Sacred Scriptures, the Scriptures of Judaism. It was clearly from Paul, however, that Timothy learned how the Sacred

whom you learned it, [15]and that from infancy you have known [the] sacred scriptures, which are capable of giving you wisdom for salvation through faith in Christ Jesus. [16]All scripture is inspired by God and is useful for teaching, for refutation, for correction, and for training in righteousness, [17]so that one who belongs to God may be competent, equipped for every good work.

Solemn Charge. [1]I charge you in the presence of God and of Christ Jesus, who will judge the living and the dead, and by his appearing and his

Scriptures could give "wisdom for salvation through faith in Christ Jesus" (3:15). How Timothy is to use the Sacred Scriptures is spelled out in the final two verses, beginning with the observation that "all scripture is inspired by God" (3:16). The more than one hundred citations of these verses in the writings of the patristic period show that they were generally understood to mean that each and every part of Scripture comes from God. At the same time, however, these writings emphasize the usefulness of Scripture far more than its inspiration and the variety of interpretive techniques used by the Fathers indicates that they had a far broader understanding of inspiration than the narrow literalism of contemporary fundamentalism.

Timothy is instructed to use the Scriptures, as Paul had, creatively guided by the Spirit, to fulfill the ministry with which he has been charged thus far in this letter. He is to use the Scriptures in teaching the sound doctrine he has received from Paul, handing it on to other faithful ministers (2:2). He is to use the Scriptures to refute the false teachers who have already become active (2:14) and whose activity will intensify in the final days (3:5). He is to use the Scriptures to correct his "opponents with kindness" when it is possible to lead them "to knowledge of the truth" (2:25). Finally, he is to use the Scriptures for training in righteousness. In order to accomplish his ministry, Timothy must himself be pure (2:22). He will then belong to God, be able to impart "the word of truth without deviation" (2:15), "be competent, equipped for every good work" (3:16; cf. 2:21).

4:1-8 Timothy's solemn commission

After the preceding sequence of instructions and exhortations, the main body of the letter comes to a close with a solemn commissioning in which Paul hands over his ministry to Timothy. The solemnity of the commissioning is emphasized by the charge being given "in the presence of God and of Christ Jesus" (4:1; cf. 1 Tim 5:21). This commissioning begins and ends with a reference to the final appearance of Christ Jesus as judge (4:1, 8), providing an eschatological context for the seriousness of Timothy's ministry.

kingly power: [2]proclaim the word; be persistent whether it is convenient or inconvenient; convince, reprimand, encourage through all patience and teaching. [3]For the time will come when people will not tolerate sound doctrine but, following their own desires and insatiable curiosity, will accumulate teachers [4]and will stop listening to the truth and will be diverted to myths. [5]But you, be self-possessed in all circumstances; put up with hardship;

Here, as earlier in the letter, the end time, "that day," is distinguished from the "last days," the dangerous times for which Timothy is now being prepared. These are the times, mentioned earlier, when "people will not tolerate sound doctrine . . . will accumulate teachers . . . and will be diverted to myths" (4:3-4; cf. 2:18; 3:6-7). Sound doctrine is a major concern throughout the Pastoral Letters, but its meaning varies. In 2 Timothy it is the words of Paul that serve as the basis for the missionary activity charged to Timothy and others (1:13; 4:3). In 1 Timothy and Titus, sound doctrine has become the moral content of Paul's gospel, involving both accuracy in teaching and the proper morality to which it leads (1 Tim 1:10; 4:6; 6:3; Titus 1:9, 13; 2:1, 2, 8).

The solemn commissioning begins with the charge "proclaim the word" (4:2). The ministry of the word is a ministry without which a Christian community cannot exist. In Acts, Paul's ministry is summarized as "preach[ing] the kingdom" (Acts 20:25; 28:31). Except for Philemon, Paul wrote about his preaching in all his letters, most eloquently in Romans 10:14-15. The charge continues with four more imperatives, all of which entail Timothy's emulating Paul and carrying on his ministry.

After a digression in which Timothy is warned about the threat of people succumbing to false teachers in the times to come (4:3-4), there is another series of four imperatives exhorting Timothy to follow Paul's example. These imperatives are introduced by "but you" (4:5), contrasting what is expected of Timothy with the expected failures of others. Timothy is to be "self-possessed in all circumstances" (4:5), a quality expected of a bishop in 1 Timothy (1 Tim 3:2). He is to "put up with hardship" (4:5), just as he had known Paul to endure persecutions and suffering (3:11). According to 1 Timothy, Christ Jesus had appointed Paul to the ministry (1 Tim 1:12). Now that Paul is about to depart, it is Timothy's turn to "perform the work of an evangelist" (4:5), a dominant theme in 2 Timothy that is all but absent in 1 Timothy and Titus. The final imperative sums up all those that have gone before and sums up the entire message of this letter: "fulfill your ministry" (4:5).

perform the work of an evangelist; fulfill your ministry.

Reward for Fidelity. ⁶For I am already being poured out like a libation, and the time of my departure is at hand. ⁷I have competed well; I have finished the race; I have kept the faith. ⁸From now on the crown of righteousness awaits me, which the Lord, the just judge, will award to me on that day, and not only to me, but to all who have longed for his appearance.

3 IV. Personal Requests and Final Greetings

Paul's Loneliness. ⁹Try to join me soon, ¹⁰for Demas, enamored of the present world, deserted me and went to

---

The message of this letter is clearly intended for all Christians of all times. The challenge to Timothy to fulfill his ministry challenges all Christians to consider the demands of their Christian vocations. For him as for all, fulfilling one's ministry involves fidelity much more than success. It involves being willing to suffer for the gospel, recognizing that the reward for fidelity is sharing in the life of the resurrection. Timothy is not urged to settle into a secure and comfortable life; rather, he and all are urged to witness, in word and deed, to the truth that is Christ in the midst of a world that prefers to follow its own desires (4:3).

The final three verses complete this final exhortation by providing the reason for the exhortation and for the letter: Paul is about to die (4:6). Just as Paul used the metaphor of athletic competition (2:5) when he urged Timothy to "bear your share of hardship" (2:3), he here applies the athletic metaphor to himself (4:7). Paul has competed well. He has kept the faith, both in the sense that he has been faithful in his office as preacher and teacher and also in the sense that he has carefully handed on the gospel and its solid doctrine to his successor. Interestingly, denial of belief in a future resurrection was the only doctrinal matter explicitly attributed to the false teachers (2:18). This autobiographical reflection fittingly ends by affirming Paul's expectation of his vindication in the future resurrection of the dead for himself as well as for all who long for the Lord's appearance (4:8).

PERSONAL POSTSCRIPT

2 Tim 4:9-18

After the conclusion of the main body of the letter, Timothy is urged four times to visit Paul (4:9, 11, 13, 21). The alleged reason is Paul's loneliness in the final days of his imprisonment before his impending death. The appeal in this section of the letter, however, provides additional

Thessalonica, Crescens to Galatia, and Titus to Dalmatia. ¹¹Luke is the only one with me. Get Mark and bring him with you, for he is helpful to me in the ministry. ¹²I have sent Tychicus to Ephesus. ¹³When you come, bring the cloak I left with Carpus in Troas, the papyrus rolls, and especially the parchments.

¹⁴Alexander the coppersmith did me a great deal of harm; the Lord will repay him according to his deeds. ¹⁵You too be on guard against him, for he has strongly resisted our preaching.

¹⁶At my first defense no one appeared on my behalf, but everyone deserted me. May it not be held against

---

biographical information about Paul, information that further supports the overall purpose of the present letter. An overarching concern of the letter is that Paul's legacy be continued (1:6; 4:1-2).

The geographical places named in this section provide a summary of the areas evangelized by Paul that now are to be cared for by his successors. Most of the persons named are associates of Paul who will be responsible for carrying on his ministry in these various regions. It is not known where Timothy presently is, but he must be somewhere other than Ephesus, otherwise he would already know that Tychicus (Titus 3:12) had been sent there (4:12).

Two of those named are cast in a negative light in ways that are significant for the letter as a whole. Demas, who was "enamored of the present world" (4:10), deserted Paul. In Acts, Demas was once a companion of Paul (Col 4:14; Phlm 24), but in the apocryphal Acts of Paul he is said to have rejected Paul's teaching on the future resurrection, saying that "it has already taken place in the children whom we have, and that we are risen again in that we have come to know the true God" (Acts of Paul 3:14). This false teaching is what led Demas to be enamored of the present world and to have deserted Paul, who is in prison and about to die. The whole thrust of 2 Timothy is toward the future resurrection which motivates the steadfastness in ministry and endurance of hardships that Paul exemplifies and which he encourages in his successors.

The other person treated negatively is Alexander the coppersmith (4:14). Just as Paul expects the Lord, the just judge, to award the crown of righteousness to himself and to "all who have longed for his appearance" (4:8), others, like Alexander, will be repaid according to their deeds. He is probably the same Alexander mentioned in 1 Timothy as an opponent of Paul (1 Tim 1:20). He is here described as having "resisted our preaching" (4:14). Timothy is warned to be on guard against him as he takes on responsibility for the ministry of preaching.

them! ¹⁷But the Lord stood by me and gave me strength, so that through me the proclamation might be completed and all the Gentiles might hear it. And I was rescued from the lion's mouth. ¹⁸The Lord will rescue me from every evil threat and will bring me safe to his heavenly kingdom. To him be glory forever and ever. Amen.

Final Greeting. ¹⁹Greet Prisca and Aquila and the family of Onesiphorus. ²⁰Erastus remained in Corinth, while I left Trophimus sick at Miletus. ²¹Try to get here before winter. Eubulus, Pudens, Linus, Claudia, and all the brothers send greetings.

²²The Lord be with your spirit. Grace be with all of you.

An interesting feature of this passage is Paul's request that Timothy bring the cloak, papyrus rolls, and parchments from Troas (4:13). The importance of the Scriptures for Timothy's ministry has already been noted (3:14-17). The cloak may be related to Elisha's succession to Elijah, which was symbolized by the assumption of his mantle (2 Kgs 2:11-14). Paul's request for his cloak and Scriptures might indicate his desire to transfer to Timothy the symbols of his ministry.

As this section draws to a close, Paul recalls his earlier trial, when everyone deserted him. He was lonely then as he is now, but then as now his strength was from the Lord. It is in this strength that he is able to say "may it not be held against them" (4:16), recalling the words of Jesus on the cross (Luke 23:34). In that earlier trial the Lord had rescued Paul (4:17), just as the Lord had rescued him in previous difficulties (3:11). This time he expects to die, but he can use the same language to describe what is to come: "the Lord will rescue me from every evil threat and will bring me safe to his heavenly kingdom" (4:18). The doxology concluding this section, like the doxologies in 1 Timothy (1 Tim 1:17; 6:15-16), contains the four elements of the classic New Testament doxology: the object of praise, "to him"; an expression of praise, "be glory"; an indication of time, "forever and ever"; and a confirmatory response, "Amen" (4:18).

THE CLOSING

2 Tim 4:19-22

As is typical in New Testament letters, the conclusion of this letter begins with a series of greetings, naming both those to be greeted, "Prisca and Aquila and the family of Onesiphorus" (4:19), as well as those in Rome sending greetings, "Eubulus, Pudens, Linus, Claudia, and all the brothers" (4:21). The closing greeting is interrupted by additional personal and place names, continuing the thoughts expressed in 4:9-13 and adding a final plea for Timothy to come to Rome (4:20-21). Prisca and Aquila were frequent coworkers with Paul (Acts 18:2; Rom 16:3; 1 Cor 16:19). Onesiphorus had served Paul both in Ephesus and Rome (1:16-18). However, none of the four sending greetings from Rome appear elsewhere in the New Testament, and their mention here is surprising, since, according to 4:11, only Luke was with Paul in his imprisonment, and Paul is pleading for Timothy to join him. Possibly they are Christians in Rome who, while not ministering to Paul in prison, will provide leadership to the Roman community after his death. Linus appears in early church traditions as the successor to Peter as leader of the church in Rome.

The letter ends with a blessing, as do all Paul's letters. Unlike the blessings at the end of 1 Timothy and Titus, this blessing is in two parts. "The Lord be with your spirit" (4:22) is in the singular, addressing Timothy, the recipient of this letter, and emphasizing the intensely personal nature of this letter. "Grace be with you all" (4:22), the blessing found at the end of 1 Timothy, is in the plural. Only these stylized closing words interrupt the letter's consistent focus on Timothy as an individual. Nevertheless, they indicate that this highly personal letter, addressed to Paul's designated successor, is intended to be read by a larger community.

The Letter to Titus

The letter to Titus is similar to 1 Timothy in content and purpose. While it is addressed to a different person, Titus, who has responsibility for a different community, Crete, it is concerned, like 1 Timothy, with pastoring the communities in the post-Pauline era. Like 1 Timothy, but unlike 2 Timothy, it provides qualifications for community leaders, codes for members of the community, and directives on ensuring that the community maintain a good reputation in the surrounding secular world. Its similarity to 1 Timothy in both language and content indicates some kind of relationship between these two letters. They may have been written by the same person or, at the very least, one was influenced by the other.

While Titus and 1 Timothy are quite similar in content and purpose, Titus addresses a situation less developed and complex than that addressed in 1 Timothy. Unlike the situation in 1 Timothy, where bishops/presbyters and deacons were already in place, in this letter Titus is charged to appoint the bishops/presbyters for the communities on Crete, a place, according to Acts, that Paul had stopped at only briefly as a prisoner on his way to Rome (Acts 27:7-15). This letter deals with a newly founded form of Christianity, unlike the situation in 1 Timothy, where it could be said that a bishop should not be a recent convert (1 Tim 3:6).

While the opponents referred to in 1 Timothy included some with Judaizing tendencies, that is, Jewish Christians who believed that Gentile converts should be made to observe Jewish religious laws and customs, in Titus the treatment of opponents is almost entirely focused on those with Judaizing tendencies (1:10, 14; 3:5, 9). The more clearly delineated threat of opponents is also more decisively dealt with. The letter to Titus links the reason for appointing leaders to the threat of Judaizing false teachers. But because the opponents threaten the good order of the community, greater emphasis is placed on behavior within the community than on the responsibilities of the newly appointed leaders. Church structures in Titus are fewer and simpler than those described in 1 Timothy, but Titus is richer in theological elaboration and the household codes are more fully developed. In this theological elaboration, Titus provides an explanation for the basis of Christian behavior, namely, the gift of God given in Christ through the power of the holy Spirit.

While Titus is the shortest of the Pastoral Letters, its opening is by far the longest. In fact, apart from that found in Romans (Rom 1:1-6), Titus's description of the sender (1:1-3) is the longest of any New Testament letter. Furthermore, this description of Paul, the sender, contains the most comprehensive description of the apostolate in the New Testament. For this reason, some suggest that Titus may have preceded 1 Timothy, introducing Paul and his apostolate and explaining how that apostolate is to be carried on by others in a particular local church setting. The present order of the Pastoral Letters in the New Testament is due to the ordering principle used at the time the scrolls of the various books were gathered together and bound into a single volume. At that time the supposed Pauline corpus was organized with the letters to churches preceding letters to individuals, and letters within these two groups organized according to length. Hence Titus was placed between 2 Timothy and Philemon.

The Letter to Titus

I. Address

1 **Greeting.** ¹Paul, a slave of God and apostle of Jesus Christ for the sake of the faith of God's chosen ones and the recognition of religious truth, ²in the hope of eternal life that God, who does not lie, promised before time began, ³who indeed at the proper time revealed his word in the proclamation with which I was entrusted by the command of God our savior, ⁴to Titus, my

1:1-4 The opening

Like most ancient letters, this letter begins with an identification of the sender and the recipient followed by a short greeting. This letter begins by identifying its sender, "Paul"; his position, "a slave of God and apostle of Christ Jesus"; and the purpose of his apostolate (1:1-3). The purpose of Paul's apostolate here, as elsewhere, involves faith in Jesus Christ. This letter and 1 Timothy, however, are concerned not only with faith but with the proper appreciation of that faith, that is, "religious truth" (1:1), which involves both correct belief and appropriate behavior. The term used here for "religious," elsewhere translated as "devoutly" (2:12), is the word used in the Roman world for reverence for the gods and respect for traditional values and practices. This much esteemed virtue receives little notice in the rest of the New Treatment but is important in Titus and especially in 1 Timothy (1 Tim 2:2; 3:16; 4:7, 8; 6:3, 5, 6, 11).

An important element in that correct belief and the motivation for appropriate behavior is the hope for a future resurrection. The letter's restrained eschatology (1:2; 2:13; 3:7) implies that the letter was written for a Christian community that no longer lived in imminent expectation of the parousia. In its more settled state, the community needed proper instruction in the fine points of Christian faith. The "hope of eternal life that God, who does not lie, promised before time began" (1:2) is what is proclaimed in the word with

▶ This symbol indicates a cross reference number in the *Catechism of the Catholic Church*. See page 79 for number citations.

Ruins of the Hercules Gate at Ephesus in Asia Minor

true child in our common faith: grace and peace from God the Father and Christ Jesus our savior.

II. Pastoral Charge

Titus in Crete. ⁵For this reason I left you in Crete so that you might set right what remains to be done and appoint presbyters in every town, as I directed you, ⁶on condition that a man be blameless, married only once, with believing children who are not accused of licentiousness or rebellious. ⁷For a bishop as God's steward must be blameless, not arrogant, not irritable, not a drunkard, not aggressive, not

which Paul has been entrusted. God our savior, "who wills everyone to be saved and to come to knowledge of the truth" (1 Tim 2:4), has entrusted this proclamation to Paul. As God's slave (1:1), Paul is bound—to fulfill his appointed task. That task involves the salvation of God's people.

The recipient is identified as "Titus, my true child in our common faith." This expression illustrates an understanding of the church as a genuinely new family that needs to be nurtured and protected as it grows and matures, as well as designating Titus as the legitimate representative authorized to minister in Paul's name. The greeting begins with the typical Pauline greeting, "grace and peace" but continues with "from God the Father and Christ Jesus our savior" (1:4).

THE NEED FOR CAPABLE, AUTHORIZED LEADERSHIP

Titus 1:5-16

1:5-9 Appointment of presbyters/bishops

Omitting the thanksgiving that is common at this point in letters (cf. 2 Tim 1:3-5), the letter identifies its purpose as charging Titus with the good order of the church at Crete. Titus's charge is twofold: to "set right what remains to be done" and to "appoint presbyters in every town" (1:5). This section dealing with "presbyters" (1:5) and a "bishop" (1:7) is the only section in the entire letter dealing with church leaders. Unlike 1 Timothy, this letter says nothing about deacons (cf. 1 Tim 3:8-13) or widows (cf. 1 Tim 5:3-10). In Titus the presbyters and bishops are clearly identical. The presbyter appointed in each town (1:5) is the bishop of that town. The term "presbyter" refers to the person's status within the community, a respected member of the community, while the term "bishop" refers to his function, exercising oversight and leadership in the community.

The list of qualifications for the presbyter/bishop in 1:6-8 is almost identical to the list of qualifications for the bishop in 1 Timothy 3:2-4. For 1 Timothy

greedy for sordid gain, ⁸but hospitable, a lover of goodness, temperate, just, holy, and self-controlled, ⁹holding fast to the true message as taught so that he will be able both to exhort with sound doctrine and to refute opponents. ¹⁰For there are also many rebels, idle talkers and deceivers, especially the Jewish Christians. ¹¹It is imperative to silence them, as they are upsetting whole families by teaching for sordid gain what they should not. ¹²One of them, a prophet of their own, once said, "Cretans have always been liars, vicious beasts, and lazy gluttons." ¹³That testimony is true. Therefore, admonish them sharply, so that they may be sound in the faith, ¹⁴instead of paying attention

---

and Titus, he must be an effective leader whose personal character is a credit to the community he leads. While the qualifications are similar to what would be expected of any reputable official in the secular world, the duties of such a leader are specific to the needs of the community, "holding fast to the true message as taught so that he will be able both to exhort with sound doctrine and to refute opponents" (1:9). These duties overlap those ascribed to presbyters in 1 Timothy, "preaching and teaching" (1 Tim 5:17), but the specific charges to exhort (1 Tim 4:13; Titus 2:15) and to refute opponents (2 Tim 2:25; Titus 2:15) are elsewhere ascribed only to Timothy and Titus.

Charging newly appointed presbyters with these responsibilities is an indication of the critical threat facing the community addressed by this letter. Throughout 1 Timothy and Titus there is a concern for sound doctrine or teaching (1 Tim 1:10; 4:6; 6:3; Titus 1:9, 13; 2:1, 2, 8), a concern related to the need for stability and order as the church faces an immediate doctrinal and moral threat. This concern should not be read, however, as a prohibition of innovative thinking, but only of erroneous teaching that harms the community. In 1 Timothy and Titus sound doctrine means the kind of well-grounded, correct doctrine that results in correct moral behavior.

1:10-16 Silencing false teachers

The first part of the charge to Titus, to "set right what remains to be done" (1:5), is what is of concern in most of the rest of this letter. Titus is here charged to do what the presbyter/bishops he appoints will be expected to do—"to refute opponents" (1:9). The immediate problem is the false teaching of the Jewish Christians, which is upsetting whole families (1:10-11). The church in Crete, which included a large number of Jewish Christians, likely encountered a problem similar to one Paul had to deal with—Gentile converts being required to observe elements of the Jewish Law like circumcision and dietary restrictions (cf. Gal 5:1-2; Phil 3:1-4). A similar problem is dealt with in 1 Timothy (1 Tim 1:7; 4:3-4). There the concern about dietary restrictions is dealt with by affirming the goodness

to Jewish myths and regulations of people who have repudiated the truth. ¹⁵To the clean all things are clean, but to those who are defiled and unbelieving nothing is clean; in fact, both their minds and their consciences are tainted. ¹⁶They claim to know God, but by their deeds they deny him. They are vile and disobedient and unqualified for any good deed.

III. Teaching the Christian Life

Christian Behavior. ¹As for yourself, you must say what is consis-

of all of God's creation, including foods and sex (1 Tim 4:4). The response in Titus, "to the clean all things are clean" (1:15) echoes the response of Paul in his letter to the Romans: "nothing is unclean in itself" (Rom 14:14).

What specifically was being taught in Crete is not clear other than that it involved "Jewish myths and regulations" (1:14) that had to do with some things being declared unclean. The false teachers are characterized as failing in one of the qualities just ascribed to a bishop, "teaching for sordid gain" (1:11; cf. 1:7; 1 Tim 3:8). In this regard they are like the false teachers dealt with in 1 Timothy, "supposing religion to be a means of gain" (1 Tim 6:5). As in 1 Timothy, the false teachers are further described as failing not only in their teaching but also in their lives (1 Tim 6:3-5). False beliefs lead to immoral behavior. "They are vile and disobedient and unqualified for any good deed" (1:16). The rhetorical device of ascribing a list of vices to the false teachers discredits these opponents. Those who had been influential insiders are now treated as outsiders.

An indication of the critical nature of the problem confronted is the harshness with which the false teachers are to be dealt. Titus and the newly appointed presbyters are to "silence them" (1:11) and "admonish them sharply" (1:13). As his mandate for dealing with issues in the community is being summed up, Titus is told to "let no one look down on you" (2:15). A similar authoritarian stance is recommended for Timothy in 1 Timothy, but it is more concerned with dealing with behavior within the community (1 Tim 4:12; 5:20) than with the threat of opponents. The harsh, authoritarian stance in both these letters contrasts with the kind and gentle approach recommended in 2 Timothy (2 Tim 2:24-26).

PROPER BEHAVIOR IN THE CHRISTIAN COMMUNITY

Titus 2:1–3:8

2:1-10 The church and social structures

Setting right what remains to be done (1:5) involves not only correct doctrine but also good order in the community that is "consistent with

tent with sound doctrine, namely, [2]that older men should be temperate, dignified, self-controlled, sound in faith, love, and endurance. [3]Similarly, older women should be reverent in their be-havior, not slanderers, not addicted to drink, teaching what is good, [4]so that they may train younger women to love their husbands and children, [5]to be self-controlled, chaste, good homemakers,

---

sound doctrine" (2:1). These verses (2:2-10) are the first part of the "household code" for the church at Crete, a code that continues at 2:15–3:3. The reason given for this code is twofold: "so that the opponent will be put to shame without anything bad to say about us" (2:8) and "so as to adorn the doctrine of God our savior in every way" (2:10). Behavior consistent with sound doctrine will adorn that doctrine, enhancing the reputation of the Christian community in the surrounding world. A radically new religious community might be suspected of being a threat to civil order. Christians behaving in accord with sound teaching will lay to rest any such concerns.

Like the household codes in 1 Timothy (2:8-15; 6:1-2, 17-19), this code pertains to the entire community as the household of God, unlike the codes in other letters that focus on the family group (Eph 5:22–6:9; Col 3:18–4:1; 1 Pet 2:13–3:8). Titus, however, goes beyond 1 Timothy in that all members of the community are not only expected to exhibit certain qualities but are also expected to play important roles in the furtherance of the community. Older men, like the bishop in 1 Timothy (1 Tim 3:2; cf. Titus 1:8), are expected to exhibit social qualities found in leading citizens; they are to be "temperate, dignified, self-controlled" (2:2). They are also to possess specific Christian virtues by being "sound in faith, love, and endurance" (2:2). Paul had identified these three virtues as the qualities in the Thessalonians for which he thanked God: "your work of faith and labor of love and endurance in hope" (1 Thess 1:3). While Paul will later place love in the final, emphatic position (1 Cor 13:13), putting "endurance in hope" last expressed his concern in his letter to the Thessalonians about life beyond the grave and the future coming of Christ. The letter to Titus is also concerned with the future coming of Christ (2:13), but here the quality in the final position is simply "endurance."

A concern for future generations is evident in the rest of this section. The qualities expected of older women are specifically intended to enable them to "train younger women" (2:4) to be good wives and mothers so that Christianity might be perceived as contributing to the stability of society (2:5). Just as Timothy is urged to "set an example for those who believe" (1 Tim 4:12), Titus himself is to serve as a model for younger men,

under the control of their husbands, so that the word of God may not be discredited.

⁶Urge the younger men, similarly, to control themselves, ⁷showing yourself as a model of good deeds in every respect, with integrity in your teaching, dignity, ⁸and sound speech that cannot be criticized, so that the opponent will be put to shame without anything bad to say about us.

⁹Slaves are to be under the control of their masters in all respects, giving them satisfaction, not talking back to them ¹⁰or stealing from them, but exhibiting complete good faith, so as to adorn the doctrine of God our savior in every way.

Transformation of Life. ¹¹For the grace of God has appeared, saving all ¹²and training us to reject godless ways and worldly desires and to live temper-

---

teaching them by word and deed to live in such a way that no one will be able to speak ill of the Christian community (2:6-8). This letter's concern that young people become respectable members of society is not found elsewhere in the New Testament but is consistent with the overall concern of 1 Timothy and Titus for the continuing life of the community.

Slaves deserve special mention (2:9-10; cf. 1 Tim 6:1-2), because in those days the vast majority of the population in urban areas were slaves. While many were well educated and some even held powerful positions, their civil status was that of slaves. Here, as elsewhere, the concern of 1 Timothy and Titus is that Christian faith should enable members of the community to become even better members of society, adhering to accepted norms of behavior, "to adorn the doctrine of God our savior in every way" (2:10).

2:11-14 Salvation

The reason for the previous household code stressing good Christian and civil behavior among all members of the community is that "the grace of God has appeared, saving all" (2:11). The verses that follow summarize Christian belief in the twofold appearance of Christ. Just as Paul is described in the identification at the start of this letter as being between the past revelation of the word and the future hope of eternal life (1:2-3), so the later Christian community lives between the two appearances of Christ. In his first appearance he saved us by his redemptive death; he "gave himself for us" (2:14). By baptism and the holy Spirit Christians are cleansed and empowered to live lives worthy of their faith as they await the future coming of Christ.

This theologically dense passage on the appearances of Christ Jesus is the most thorough treatment of the basic Christian kerygma in the Pas-

ately, justly, and devoutly in this age, ¹³as we await the blessed hope, the appearance of the glory of the great God and of our savior Jesus Christ, ¹⁴who gave himself for us to deliver us from all lawlessness and to cleanse for himself a people as his own, eager to do what is good.

¹⁵Say these things. Exhort and correct with all authority. Let no one look down on you.

3 ¹Remind them to be under the control of magistrates and authorities, to be obedient, to be open to every good enterprise. ²They are to slander no one, to be peaceable, considerate,

---

toral Letters. Unlike 1 Timothy, which speaks only of the end-time appearance of Christ Jesus, Titus stresses both Christ's future appearance (1:13) and the salvific nature of his past appearance (2:11; 3:4). Unlike 1 Timothy, where only God is called "savior" (1 Tim 1:1; 2:3; 4:10), in Titus the term is used both for God (1:3; 2:10; 3:4) and Christ (1:4; 2:13; 3:6), although the two are clearly differentiated in 1:3-4 and 3:4-6. God is the source of hope insofar as he saves us by being faithful to his promises, sending Christ Jesus to redeem us and form us into his chosen people (2:14). We are saved by the past appearance of Christ, but it is the future appearance that is the source of the hope (2:13) that is the basis for the household code. While future hope is more prominent in Titus (1:2; 2:13; 3:7), this same theological foundation is found in 1 Timothy, though it is not as fully expressed in that letter (1 Tim 2:3-6).

2:15–3:3 Exhortation to good citizenship

The household code (2:1-10), interrupted by providing its theological foundation (2:11-14), is here concluded by explicitly charging Titus to exhort the community to good citizenship. "These things" (2:15) that Titus is to say are the things he is told to say in 2:1-10. He is further charged to "exhort and correct" (2:15), doing what the presbyter/bishop he will appoint will be expected to do (1:9). Furthermore, he is told to "let no one look down on you" (2:15), just as Timothy was told to "let no one have contempt for your youth" (1 Tim 4:12). Both Timothy and Titus are presented in these letters as younger companions of Paul who are placed in positions of authority in their respective communities.

After the personal charge to Titus, the preceding household code is then summarized in terms that make explicit that, as a whole, it is to be understood as a charge to good citizenship. The "them" in 3:1 refers to all those whose behavior was commented on in chapter 2. In 1 Timothy, Christians were urged to pray "for kings and for all in authority" (1 Tim 2:2). Here they are to be "under the control of magistrates and authorities"

exercising all graciousness toward everyone. ³For we ourselves were once foolish, disobedient, deluded, slaves to various desires and pleasures, living in malice and envy, hateful ourselves and hating one another.

⁴But when the kindness and
generous love
of God our savior appeared,

⁵not because of any righteous deeds
we had done
but because of his mercy,
he saved us through the bath of
rebirth
and renewal by the holy Spirit,
⁶whom he richly poured out on us
through Jesus Christ our savior,
⁷so that we might be justified by his
grace

(3:1). The charge to obey civil authority is found elsewhere in the New Testament (Rom 13:1-7; 1 Pet 2:13-17), but in 1 Timothy and Titus it is integral to the moral exhortations throughout the letters. These letters urge Christians to participate fully in civic life through gainful employment, respect for neighbors, and obedience to civil authority.

3:4-8 Baptismal hymn

These verses contain language used nowhere else in the Pastoral Letters, most likely because they are part of a preexisting hymn. The previous passage on salvation (2:11-14) offered a kind of commentary on this hymn and provided the theological basis for the exhortation in the household code. Now the letter presents the hymn itself, labeling it as a trustworthy saying (3:8; cf. 1 Tim 1:15; 3:1; 4:9; 2 Tim 2:11), a phrase regularly used in the Pastoral Letters to identify a basic truth of early Christian faith.

The present passage provides a brief synthesis of Pauline theology. Apart from Romans 6:3-11, it contains the most important statement on baptism in the New Testament. Through baptism Christians are no longer slaves to sin but are reborn by the holy Spirit as heirs in hope of eternal life. This hymn situates its teaching on baptism in the context of the two appearances of Christ, the context for all the exhortations of Titus. It further presents the Pauline teaching on justification as the basis for the baptismal lives now led in hope. The use of this hymn allows the letter to Titus to connect its treatment of the Jewish Christian problem to that confronted by Paul. In Galatians and again in Romans, Paul confronted those who felt that people could be saved by their own righteous deeds. For Paul as well as for the letter to Titus, people are "justified by his grace" (3:7) and not by "any righteous deeds" (3:5).

The previous passage on salvation (2:11-14) explained what is involved in living lives based on baptismal conversion, denying impiety and worldly passions while living modestly, justly and piously and wait-

and become heirs in hope of eternal life.

[8]This saying is trustworthy.

Advice to Titus. I want you to insist on these points, that those who have believed in God be careful to devote themselves to good works; these are excellent and beneficial to others. [9]Avoid foolish arguments, genealogies, rivalries, and quarrels about the law, for they are useless and futile. [10]After a first and second warning, break off contact with a heretic, [11]realizing that such a person is perverted and sinful and stands self-condemned.

Directives, Greetings, and Blessing. [12]When I send Artemas to you, or Tychicus, try to join me at Nicopolis,

---

ing in hope for the appearance of Christ. This hymn makes explicit the early Christian teaching that baptismal lives are led by the power of the holy Spirit. Only here and in 2 Timothy 1:14 is the role of the holy Spirit in Christian living explicitly mentioned in the Pastoral Letters. While teachings about the holy Spirit are not emphasized in these letters, the theological concerns of these letters are firmly grounded in the early traditions about the holy Spirit.

FINAL DIRECTIVES TO TITUS

Titus 3:8-11

As the letter draws to a close, the main points of the letter are summarized. What Titus was told to say in chapter 2 (2:1, 15) he is here told to insist on, that is, that people do good and avoid evil (3:8-9). Avoiding evil involves specifically the kinds of evil promoted by the Judaizing opponents at Crete (1:10-16), like arguing about genealogies. The tasks assigned to bishops and to Titus as well, to exhort and refute opponents (1:9; 2:15), are here given further specification, consistent with what Paul is said to have done in 1 Timothy (1 Tim 1:20). Excommunication is to be used as a last resort in dealing with one who upsets the community. Calling the person a "heretic" and further pointing out that the person is "perverted and sinful and stands self-condemned" (3:10-11) gives expression to the overall perspective of 1 Timothy and Titus, linking belief, true or false, with behavior, good or bad.

FINAL REMARKS AND FAREWELL

Titus 3:12-15

Mention of travel plans is a common feature at the end of Paul's letters. Here the mention of travel plans, those of Paul and of others, are presented

Titus 3:13-15

where I have decided to spend the winter. [13]Send Zenas the lawyer and Apollos on their journey soon, and see to it that they have everything they need. [14]But let our people, too, learn to devote themselves to good works to supply urgent needs, so that they may not be unproductive.

[15]All who are with me send you greetings. Greet those who love us in the faith.

Grace be with all of you.

---

in a way that illustrates authorization for ministry, one of the overarching concerns of 1 Timothy and Titus. Paul is now about to send either Artemis or Tychicus to Crete to replace Titus while Titus visits Paul at Nicopolis (3:12). In 2 Timothy 4:12, Paul had sent Tychicus to Ephesus. Just as Paul has sent Titus, Timothy, and others to administer churches, Titus in now charged to send others, Zenas and Apollos, to exercise their ministries in other places (3:13). They, like Titus and Timothy, are to devote themselves to their ministries (3:14; cf. 1 Tim 4:6, 16; 2 Tim 2:15; 4:2; Titus 1:5). While verse 14 continues the instruction on the two missionaries, the phrase "our people" can be understood as applying to the entire community.

The letter concludes with a greeting and a final blessing, both typical of the way Paul concludes his letters. While the greeting is addressed to Titus ("you" in the singular), who is then to extend Paul's greeting to others, the blessing is addressed to "all of you," an indication that the blessing and indeed the entire letter is intended not for a single person, Titus, but for the whole church.

The Letter to Philemon

The letter to Philemon is the shortest but one of the most intriguing letters in the New Testament. Almost all scholars agree that it was written by Paul himself during one of his imprisonments. It provides one piece of an extended conversation involving Paul, Onesimus, Philemon, and others. The information the other parts of the conversation would provide remain a mystery and have been the subject of much conjecture. Fortunately most of this missing information, while interesting, is not crucial for appreciating the ongoing significance of this short and beautiful letter.

Paul is clearly in prison at the time of the letter, but the where and when of the imprisonment are not known. Discussions on these questions are usually linked to discussion about his imprisonment at the time he wrote his letter to the Philippians, and answers vary widely. Were both letters written from Rome and hence later than the letter to the Romans? Were one or both written from Ephesus or some other location? Was one written from an earlier or later imprisonment than the other? It seems most likely but hardly certain that Philemon was written during an earlier imprisonment, possibly at Ephesus, from which Paul expected to be released, and hence be able to visit Philemon and continue his ministry. Travel for both Onesimus and Paul from Ephesus to Colossae, the usually assumed location of Philemon's home, would be relatively easy, since they are only about a hundred miles apart.

Onesimus is a slave belonging to Philemon and is, at the time of the letter, with Paul. Why he has left his owner and is with Paul is also the subject of much speculation. He has done something to offend his owner, which could have been some inappropriate act while he was in his service or which may simply have been his running away. While he may have been a runaway slave, the prevailing opinion is that he was visiting Paul to appeal to him for advice and assistance in his difficulty with his owner. Some have even suggested that Philemon sent his pagan slave to minister to Paul in prison. It is also not certain what Paul expects Philemon to do. He is clearly asking him to receive Onesimus back as a brother in the Lord and to charge Paul for whatever debt Onesimus owes. Paul, however, also says that he would like Onesimus to be able to serve him and seems to be suggesting that Philemon do even more than he is explicitly asked to do, perhaps even give Onesimus to Paul as his slave.

This letter, like others in the New Testament, simply accepts slavery as an institution without discussing its morality. This letter does, however, recognize the tension that exists between the liberating message of the gospel (cf. Gal 3:26-28; 1 Cor 12:13) and the slavery that society accepted. In its treatment of Christian brotherly love, it provides a basis for later Christian understanding of the slavery issue. It calls for a reordering of relationships on a higher plane than those possible within secular society. While many questions will remain unanswered, the letter to Philemon can be read by Christians of all ages as an exposition on the new relationship that exists among people as a result of their incorporation into Christ. This relationship, which transcends all other relationships, including that of master and slave, is based on the new life that all Christians share by reason of the grace that comes from Christ. This new life involves both mutual love and partnership in promoting the gospel.

The Letter to Philemon

Address and Greeting. ¹Paul, a
prisoner for Christ Jesus, and Timothy
our brother, to Philemon, our beloved
and our co-worker, ²to Apphia our sister, to Archippus our fellow soldier,
and to the church at your house. ³Grace

THE OPENING

Phlm 1-3

1-2 Senders and recipients

Like all Paul's letters, the letter to Philemon opens by identifying both
the senders and the recipients. The senders are Paul and Timothy. Elsewhere Paul calls himself "an apostle of Christ Jesus" (1 Cor 1:1) or "a slave
of Christ Jesus" (Rom 1:1), but here he identifies himself a "a prisoner for
Christ Jesus" (1). This identification refers not only to his actual status as a
prisoner but even more to the reason for his being a prisoner—his preaching of the gospel of Christ—and most especially, in the context of the purpose of this letter, to Christ's total, authoritative claim on Paul and Paul's
dedication to that claim. Timothy's being called a "brother" establishes
his close relationship with Paul and also prepares for Paul's addressing
Philemon as "brother" (7, 20) and his appealing to Philemon to accept
Onesimus as a "brother" (16).

The main recipient of the letter is Philemon, but the letter is also addressed to other key individuals in his community, Appia and Archippus,
and to the whole community. In the early church, communities were usually small enough to gather for worship in a private home, often that of a
leading citizen like Philemon. While the immediate purpose of the letter is
to persuade Philemon to do a good deed, the argument of the letter involves Philemon's understanding of his and Onesimus's relationship
within the whole community. Using the terms "brother" and "sister" as

---

▶ This symbol indicates a cross reference number in the *Catechism of the Catholic Church*. See
page 79 for number citations.

to you and peace from God our Father and the Lord Jesus Christ.

Thanksgiving. [4]I give thanks to my God always, remembering you in my prayers, [5]as I hear of the love and the faith you have in the Lord Jesus and for all the holy ones, [6]so that your partnership in the faith may become effective in recognizing every good there is in us that leads to Christ.

---

well as "co-worker" sets the stage for the new relationship Paul seeks to bring about between Philemon and Onesimus. Addressing the letter to the whole community provides greater incentive for Philemon to comply with the letter's request. It also gives the letter applicability, beyond Philemon himself, to the whole community as well as to Christian communities of future generations.

3 Greeting

The formal greeting is similar to those used in Paul's other letters and has the same wording as the greeting in Paul's other letter from prison (Phil 1:2). While formal, this greeting, together with the formal blessing at the end (25), frames the body of the letter within the context of God's grace. Paul's theology of grace is nowhere developed in this letter, nor are other aspects of his theology. It is reasonable to assume, however, that Philemon and his community, having been converted by Paul, are familiar with the main aspects of Paul's teaching. God's graciousness toward Philemon and his community should inspire their graciousness toward one another.

THANKSGIVING

Phlm 4-7

4-5 Philemon's love and faith

The thanksgiving, which follows the opening greeting in all Paul's letters except Galatians, usually involves thanking God for some quality in the letter's recipient and serves to introduce the main themes of the letter. Here Paul thanks God for Philemon's love and faith, qualities that will be the basis of Paul's appeal in the body of the letter. Paul sees in Philemon's faith not just his assent to the gospel but the way his vital faith has been operative in his life— "faith working through love" (Gal 5:6). Philemon's love "for all the holy ones" (5) includes those in "the church at your house" (2), Paul himself (7), and will shortly be extended to include Onesimus (16).

6-7 Effects of Philemon's love and faith

In the opening of the letter, Paul referred to Philemon as "our co-worker" (1). He now strengthens that designation by referring to him as

Plea for Onesimus. ⁷For I have experienced much joy and encouragement from your love, because the hearts of the holy ones have been refreshed by you, brother. ⁸Therefore, although I have the full right in Christ to order you to do what is proper, ⁹I rather urge you out of love, being as I am, Paul, an old man, and now also a prisoner for Christ Jesus. ¹⁰I urge you on

---

"brother" (7), associating him more closely with himself and with "Timothy our brother" (1), the co-author of the letter. Paul suggests that he and Philemon together can now do even more good for the holy ones than what Paul has already seen Philemon doing. Thus far, Paul has drawn an extremely positive picture of Philemon. As the letter develops, Philemon will be expected to live up to this positive picture. The themes of prayer (4), love (5, 7), partnership (6), good (6), and refreshing the heart (7) will all be used as Paul develops his argument.

APPEAL ON BEHALF OF ONESIMUS

Phlm 8-21

8-12 Paul appeals out of love

Paul claims the right to order Philemon to do the good he is about to propose, but refrains from exercising this right. This right probably derives from Paul's apostolic authority, although Paul called himself a prisoner rather than an apostle in the introduction to the letter. Because of the encouragement he has felt on the basis of the good that has come from Philemon's love, rather than order him to do what is proper, Paul urges him "out of love" (9). The love here referred to is both Philemon's love for all the holy ones (5) and Paul's and Timothy's love for Philemon (1). Paul refers to himself as an old man and as a prisoner (9) as motivation for Philemon to extend to Paul the love he has for the holy ones.

Having established the basis of his appeal as the love relationship that exists between himself and Philemon and their mutual love for the holy ones, Paul now identifies the object of his appeal. Whatever he may have been, Onesimus has become Paul's child in prison. By bringing him into Christianity, Paul has become his "father." Paul will describe him as "my own heart" (12). Onesimus has become one of the holy ones mutually loved by Paul and Philemon. Significantly, the term "child," which Paul uses to refer to Onesimus and often to Christians in general, is used in his letters for only one other individual, namely, Timothy (1 Cor 4:17; Phil 2:22), Paul's partner in spreading the gospel and a co-author of this letter.

behalf of my child Onesimus, whose father I have become in my imprisonment, ¹¹who was once useless to you but is now useful to [both] you and me. ¹²I am sending him, that is, my own heart, back to you. ¹³I should have liked to retain him for myself, so that he might serve me on your behalf in my imprisonment for the gospel, ¹⁴but I did not want to do anything without your consent, so that the good you do might not be forced but voluntary. ¹⁵Perhaps

---

The extensive use of family language in this letter indicates that a new model of mutual relationships has already been established within the Christian community, a model of relationships that is in tension with the master/slave relationship accepted in Roman society. Paul does not advocate the overthrow of the institution of slavery, but he does advocate overcoming the tension by fully incorporating the Christian slave into the familial relationships within the Christian community. In at least two ways Paul has described a new household in tension with the structured household of Philemon. First, in this new household Paul, not Philemon, is the head; both Philemon and Onesimus are his children. Second, Paul's father/child relationship with Onesimus has priority over Philemon's master/slave relationship with Onesimus.

The name Onesimus, a common name for slaves, means "the useful one," enabling the play on words in verse 11. Away from Philemon, Onesimus was useless to him. Now a Christian devoted to Paul, he has become useful both to Paul and to Philemon. He will become useful to Philemon when Paul sends him back, but his real usefulness to both Philemon and Paul will become clear later in the letter.

13-14 Philemon's voluntary good deed

Paul never explicitly states what it is that he expects Philemon to do. He had said that he had a right "to order you to do what is proper" (8), but here says he wants the good Philemon will do to be voluntary (14), a good deed on the part of Philemon in response to the grace of God. He says he would have liked Onesimus to remain with him, serving him in prison for the gospel, an indication that Onesimus, like many slaves at that time, was well educated and hence equipped to be of service to Paul and the gospel. However, he sends him back to Philemon and apparently expects Onesimus to be with Philemon when he is released from prison and visits Philemon (22).

15-18 Paul's request

Paul appears to be asking Philemon to receive his slave back, charging Paul for anything that Onesimus might owe as a result of previous

this is why he was away from you for a while, that you might have him back forever, [16]no longer as a slave but more than a slave, a brother, beloved especially to me, but even more so to you, as a man and in the Lord. [17]So if you regard me as a partner, welcome him as you would me. [18]And if he has done

---

misdeeds or his temporary absence. Paul, however, is asking for much more. He is asking that Philemon receive Onesimus back not only as a slave but also as a brother in the Lord. He is asking that he receive Onesimus both as a man, that is, as a fellow Christian who is his slave, and in the Lord, that is, as a co-worker in the gospel. Most of all, Paul is asking that Philemon receive Onesimus back just as warmly as he would welcome Paul. Onesimus has become Paul's "own heart" (12). Just as Philemon is Paul's co-worker in the gospel (1), so too Philemon should regard Onesimus as a co-worker, like Paul, in the gospel. Verse 17 implies that Paul's primary concern was to effect a reconciliation between Philemon and Onesimus.

Modern readers are often disappointed that Paul does not ask Philemon to grant freedom to his slave. While some scholars think that there are passages (16, 21) that can be read as hinting that Paul desires Onesimus's freedom, most do not, and all agree that the letter falls far short of reconsidering the practice of slavery. In fact, recent studies in cultural anthropology have shown that Philemon's simply freeing his slave would not have fundamentally altered his relationships within the household. Paul wants to alter these relationships. The letter offers a model for transforming the way Christians view one another, now seeing other human beings with eyes reconditioned by faith in Jesus Christ. The transforming power of God's grace, personally experienced by Paul, led to his conviction about God's ability to make all things new (2 Cor 5:17). Paul was actually asking Philemon for something far more radical than freeing his slave. Paul's declaration that Onesimus is Philemon's brother both "as a man and in the Lord" (16) indicates not merely a spiritual reevaluation in the sight of the Lord but a real change in the social relationship between slave and owner.

As the father of Onesimus (10), Paul now accepts responsibility for the debts of his son. In so accepting this responsibility, however, Paul is emphasizing the intensity of his relationship with Onesimus and setting the stage for the implied request at the end of the letter. Martin Luther saw in Paul's letter to Philemon a parallel to the kenotic hymn Paul quotes in Philippians (Phil 2:6-11), his other letter from prison. Christ emptied him-

you any injustice or owes you anything, charge it to me. [19]I, Paul, write this
in my own hand: I will pay. May I not
tell you that you owe me your very self.

[20]Yes, brother, may I profit from you in
the Lord. Refresh my heart in Christ.

[21]With trust in your compliance I
write to you, knowing that you will do

---

self of his right with the Father and instead died to bring us into favor
with God. As Christ pleads our cause and takes our part, so too Paul has
emptied himself of his rights and takes the place of Onesimus in order to
get Philemon to waive his right to punish Onesimus and instead welcome
him as a brother.

19-21 Personal appeal

Paul's letters were dictated by him and written by a scribe, but he
would sometimes add a note at the end in his "own hand" (19; cf. 1 Cor
16:21; Gal 6:11). By writing in his own hand he is concluding his appeal by
making his request intensely personal. He now not only restates his agree-
ment to pay Onesimus's debt but also reminds Philemon of the debt he
owes to Paul. The new life in Christ that Philemon now lives he owes to
Paul, that is, he owes Paul his "very self" (19). With this comment Paul
draws Philemon into the creditor-debtor relationship as a debtor as well
as a creditor. The sphere of mutual relationships is expanded. Philemon,
in fact, has the same relationship to Paul as does Onesimus. For both, Paul
is their father in faith. For both, Paul is their partner in the gospel (1; 13).

Paul is expecting Philemon to reflect on the significance of these relationships when Paul asks to "profit from you in the Lord" (20), followed
by his appeal to Philemon to "refresh my heart in Christ" (20). Paul is expecting Philemon to reflect on his love for Paul and his partnership with
him in the gospel and to consider what he can do to further support him
in his ministry. Near the beginning of the letter Paul thanked God for
Philemon's love, faith, and partnership, noting that "the hearts of the holy
ones have been refreshed by you" (7). He identified Onesimus as "my
own heart" (12) and now asks Philemon to "refresh my heart" (20). Paul
concludes this personal appeal by expressing his confidence that Philemon
will not only do what Paul has explicitly asked, that is, receive Onesimus
back as a brother in the Lord, but will do even more (21).

Paul is certainly expecting that Philemon will accept Onesimus not
only as a returned slave and a brother in the Lord but also as a beloved co-
worker in the gospel, a partner with Paul and Philemon. He may also be
expecting that Philemon will refresh his heart by granting the wish Paul
had earlier expressed: "that he might serve me on your behalf" (13).

even more than I say. ²²At the same time prepare a guest room for me, for I hope to be granted to you through your prayers.
Final Greetings. ²³Epaphras, my fel- low prisoner in Christ Jesus, greets you, ²⁴as well as Mark, Aristarchus, Demas, and Luke, my co-workers. ²⁵The grace of the Lord Jesus Christ be with your spirit.

Philemon indeed may have Onesimus back forever by giving him to Paul as their mutual partner in the gospel.

This letter calls not only Philemon but all Christians to adopt new patterns of mutual respect, mutual responsibility, and mutual concern. This letter can help Christian communities today to reflect on the roles and concerns of minorities and others who might be marginalized. Accepting the transforming power of God's grace will not only alter relationships but can offer new possibilities for living out Christian faith in freedom and joy.

CONCLUSION

Phlm 22-25

22 Travel plans

Travel plans are a common feature of Paul's letters, appearing just before the final greetings and blessing. Here Paul indicates his hope to be able to visit Philemon. There must have been a realistic prospect of his being released from prison, a development for which he asks the prayers of Philemon and his community. His arrival at the home of Philemon would be an appropriate occasion for Philemon to refresh his heart by granting him Onesimus. To this point in the letter, "you" has been in the singular, referring to Philemon alone. The request for prayers, however, uses "your" in the plural, indicating not only that Paul is asking for the prayers of the community but also that this personal letter to Philemon is intended to be read to the entire community.

23-25 Greeting and blessing

Greetings are another common feature of Paul's letters, appearing just before the final blessing. The greetings from Paul's fellow prisoner, Epaphras, and four fellow workers are addressed to "you" in the singular, that is, to Philemon alone, possibly because they were personally known by Philemon. The final blessing, however, is addressed to the entire community, using the blessing formula similar to those found in Paul's other letters and identical to that in Paul's other letter from prison, the letter to the Philippians (Phil 4:23).

REVIEW AIDS AND DISCUSSION TOPICS

I Timothy *(pages 5–32)*

1. In the Introduction, the author discusses why most scholars believe 1 and 2 Timothy and Titus were not written by Paul. Do you think these reasons are convincing? Why? What are some of the specific reasons given for 1 Timothy?

2. In chapter 1, what is Timothy's primary duty according to the author? In what context is this duty to be discharged? What doctrine is at the heart of Paul's gospel ("this saying is true"), entrusted to Timothy and through him to the community? How do you, as a member of the Christian community, convey to people the doctrine at the heart of Paul's gospel?

3. How are we to assess the material about women in 2:9-15? Is this the only teaching about the social role of women in the New Testament? Is this normative for all women, everywhere, at all times? How can we responsibly critique these ideas and arguments?

4. Do the qualifications for bishops/presbyters and deacons essentially differ from those expected of pagan and Jewish officials? What is the author's purpose in requiring these qualifications, which are not specifically Christian? Do you think these qualifications help officials to make known to the world the message of salvation for all? Why?

5. Does the author's emphasis on Christians' being good citizens of the Empire agree with Jesus' life and preaching in the gospels? Why?

6. Does what the author says about wealth agree with what Jesus says about wealth in the Gospels (Matt 19:16-30; Mark 10:2-31; Luke 18:18-30)? Why?

2 Timothy *(pages 33–53)*

1. This letter is often considered Paul's last will and testament. What passages does this refer to? How would this help us to explain the function of the letter in the light of the historical needs of this church?

2. Who are Lois and Eunice (1:5), and why does Paul mention them? How does their relationship to Timothy parallel Paul's own relationship to him? Compare their importance here with the role of women in 1 Tim 2:11-14 and 5:3-16.

3. What are the various meanings of faith in 2 Timothy? Which ones are most central to the main themes of the letter? Why is there this particular stress?

4. How does the hymn about Jesus in 2:11-13 relate to the main themes of the letter? Why was this particular hymn chosen?

5. There is a surprisingly large amount of talk about the day of judgment and rewards/punishments in 2 Timothy. Why is this so pastorally important to this letter? What is the pastoral importance of stressing Jesus' "coming to judge" in 4:1-8? Is this a threat to Timothy? Is it a statement of consolation? Do you feel it as a personal threat or consolation? Why?

6. Compare the tasks of ministry assigned to Timothy with those enjoined on the apostles in Jesus' last will and testament in Luke 22:24-27. Why the difference? What is the situation of the church of Timothy which requires so strict a view? Is this the only way to exercise ministry in the church?

Titus *(pages 54–66)*

1. Why does Titus have to appoint presbyters/bishops? What qualities are they to possess and are they different from those of reputable officials in the secular world? What are their duties?

2. What critical problem faces the church in Crete? How are Titus and the presbyters/bishops he appoints to deal with it? How are they to deal with the "false teachers"? Why is the punishment so harsh?

3. In the list of household duties, was the church presenting itself as a revolutionary group? Why or why not? Did the church, according to Titus, ignore social structures?

4. What is the advantage of being a Christian in Titus? According to 3:3-8, does Christianity make a difference in our lives? What does being a Christian mean to you? Are there times when obeying civil or ecclesiastical authorities may be contrary to your being faithful to your Christian faith?

Philemon *(pages 67–75)*

1. Why is Paul in prison at the time of this letter and why is he writing to Philemon? Is Philemon an important person in the church to which he belongs? Why? Is the letter a purely "personal" one? Why?

2. What is the specific request Paul makes of Philemon? In what ways does Paul use his powers of persuasion? Do you find them effective?

3. How does the letter deal with the issue of slavery?

4. If Paul is asking for a radical change, for a real change in the social relationship between slave and owner, for the owner to receive the slave as a human being and brother or sister in the Lord, what does that say to us as members of the Christian community? What does that say to us about our relationships to members of our parish church with whom we need to be reconciled, to whom we've not spoken for years? What does it say about our relationship to those beyond our community, beyond our church, beyond our religion?

INDEX OF CITATIONS FROM THE
CATECHISM OF THE CATHOLIC CHURCH

The arabic number(s) following the citation refer to the paragraph number(s) in the *Catechism of the Catholic Church*. The asterisk following a paragraph number indicates that the citation has been paraphrased.

1 Timothy		5:17-18	2122*	2:23-26	2518*
1:3-4	2518*	6:8	2837*	3:2-5	1852*
1:5	1794	6:12	2145*	3:12	2847*
1:9-10	1852*	6:15-16	2641*	4	2015*
1:10	2357*	6:16	52	4:1	679*
1:15	545*	6:20	84*		
1:18-19	162			**Titus**	
2:1-2	1349, 1900*	**2 Timothy**		1:5-9	1577*
2:1	2636	1:3	1794*	1:5	1590
2:2	2240	1:5	2220	1:15	2518*
2:3-4	2822	1:6	1577,* 1590	2:1-6	2342*
2:4	74, 851, 1058,	1:8	2471, 2506	2:12	1809
	1256,* 1261,* 1821	1:9-10	257, 1021*	2:13	449,* 1041,
2:5-8	2634*	1:12-14	84*		1130, 1404,*
2:5	618, 1544, 2574	1:12	149		2760, 2818*
3:1-13	1577	1:13-14	857*	2:14	802
3:1	1590	1:14	1202	3:5	1215
3:9	1794*	2:5	1264	3:6-7	1817
3:15	171, 756,* 2032	2:8	437*		
3:16	385, 463, 2641*	2:11-13	2641*	**Philemon**	
4:1	672*	2:11	1010	16	2414
4:3-9	2518*	2:22	2518*		

The World of Paul

Black Sea

Byzantium

ITALIA

Rome

MACEDONIA
Philippi
Thessalonica
Beroea
ACHAIA

Aegean Sea

Troas

ASIA

Ephesus

Athens
Corinth

MALTA

CRETE

Mediterranean Sea

GALATIA

Antioch
Iconium
Lystra
Colossus

LYCIA
Myra
Perga

CILICIA
Tarsus

RHODES

Antioch

CYPRUS
Paphos

SYRIA
Sidon
Damascus
Tyre
Ptolemais
Caesarea
Antipatris
Joppa
Jerusalem

Alexandria

200 km

0

100 miles

0